Smart Money
In
Hard Times

Smart Money
in
Hard Times

A Guide to
Inflationproof Investments

---

by Ronald L. Soble

McGraw-Hill Book Company

New York   St. Louis   San Francisco   Auckland   Dusseldorf
Johannesburg   Kuala Lumpur   London   Mexico   Montreal
New Delhi   Panama   Paris   Sao Paulo   Singapore
Sydney   Tokyo   Toronto

Library of Congress Cataloging in Publication Data

Soble, Ronald L
  Smart money in hard times.

  Includes index.
  1. Investments. I. Title.
HG4521.S7115   332.6   74-23560
ISBN 0-07-059562-3

1234567890 BPBP 784321098765

For Anne and Mark Soble
and Bernard Gagan

PUBLISHER'S NOTE

The purpose of this book is to present the author's views on how to invest during times of high inflation. The author is not giving legal advice. If the investor has any questions about an investment, consultation should be made either with a member of the financial community or a lawyer. The author is not responsible for changes in government policy or that of private industry which could alter the contents of this book.

CONTENTS

INTRODUCTION

There's no set formula for becoming rich. When someone writes a surefire bestseller on how to make a killing in the stock market or soybean futures or whatever, you're only getting their theory, which is subject to a thousand imponderables. If that wasn't so, the sharing of this knowledge would make us all rich.

The most a financial journalist such as myself can do is to outline options open to the investor. I make no specific recommendations on how to structure your investment portfolio. That decision must be yours after analyzing your finances and the channels of investment which you wish to pursue.

What I do lay out for study are some forms of investment designed to meet the high inflation times in which we live. Hopefully, these ideas will expand your investment horizons. I cannot, however, play the role of the financial wizard who has all the answers.

But there's no reason why you shouldn't try to get the most out of life even during difficult economic times. Investment ideas contained in this book will help you achieve this objective.

Chapter I

IS DOOMSDAY AROUND THE CORNER?

—Inflation and Investment, an Introduction

"The country's going to pot."

So observed Soames Forsyte of Galsworthy's *Forsyte Saga.*

Old Soames' remark is being echoed with increasing frequency these days. The villain is inflation. And it's the biggest scandal and the most serious crisis the United States has ever faced.

Oh, sure, we had Watergate and its implications of moral breakdown among those we elected to high public office and the bureaucrats they selected to help them carry out their political skulduggery.

But the Watergates—as this one did—pass away. They are a fact of life, symptomatic of the greed and arrogance of politics. Watergate was a product of a free and competitive society where there is plenty of room for corruption. To be sure, there have been undetected Watergates, perhaps on a smaller scale, in both the political and economic history of the United States. In *the* Watergate affair, however, too many hands got caught in the till. Suddenly, President Richard M. Nixon found himself backed into a corner and had to resign.

But Watergate didn't alter the way we conduct our day-to-day lives. Watergate's rascals were run out of Washington and the political process under the new Administration of President Gerald R. Ford had an opportunity to open fresh political lines of communication with the American people.

Soon, Watergate's ramifications will be forgotten by the New York accountant, the Kansas wheat farmer, and the California shoe salesman. But, as the new Ford Administration well knows, a much bigger scandal that was mounting before Watergate isn't about to be forgotten by the man on the street. That's because it directly affects the way we lead our daily lives.

That scandal is the inability of the United States government to control mounting inflation.

At this writing the inflation picture is bleak. A once optimistic Nixon Administration had suggested that high levels of inflation would continue for the foreseeable future. The Ford Administration, pledging, of course, to fight inflation, didn't improve upon this forecast.

To Mr. Ford's credit, however, he recognized the nature of the problem at the outset of his Presidency and put it into perspective.

Mr. Ford, in his first address to a joint session of Congress on August 12, 1974, following Mr. Nixon's resignation amid the Watergate revelations, declared:

"My first priority is to work with you to bring inflation under control. Inflation is our domestic public enemy number one. To restore economic confidence, the government in Washington must provide leadership. It does no good to blame the public for spending too much when the government is spending too much."

The unprecedented prolonged high consumer price inflation level (aggravated by the energy shortage) leaped to 15.1% in the first quarter of 1974 and only slightly improved to 13.2% for the second quarter. The consumer price index wasn't retreating according to plan. The cost of food, health services, and the rest of life's necessities continued to rise. And interest rates, reflecting inflationary demand, had reached double-digit levels for the first time in history.

Inflation is painful. It hurts where we are most vulnerable—in the pocketbook. It's unfair because it hits hardest those who can least afford it. It profoundly affects how we live, how we eat, and, in short, how we cope with our daily lives.

If left unchecked, soaring inflation is the one major infection that can bring the powerful United States to its knees.

Inflation—not Watergate—is the scandal of the decade.

* * *

Henry Kaufman, the astute economist with Salomon Brothers, the New York investment banking firm, says: "Government officials have described the recent rapid increase in prices as being to a large extent beyond the responsibility and control of government. Their description even tends to hint that much of what has happened was somehow an act of God.

"The fact of the matter still is, however, that the price performance during the past three years is by far the worst for all postwar economic expansions, and that our government must be held largely responsible."

Kaufman, as well as others who have an understanding of the destructive forces of inflation, attribute the current situation to the overly stimulative monetary policies of the Federal Reserve Board, which is the U.S. central bank.

And, they say, the fiscal side was just as disastrous with the Nixon Administration accumulating $65 billion worth of budget deficits in four years.

In that address to the joint Congressional session, Mr. Ford promised to strive for a balanced Federal budget in fiscal year 1976, which is the financial year starting on July 1, 1975.

The trouble is, note many economy-watchers, that the budget must be balanced now, not at some nebulous date in the near future. "We have a crisis now," one Wall Streeter grumbled after the Ford speech. "We need action now, not next year." Obviously, Mr. Ford is attempting to dampen inflation's fires as soon as possible. But as each month goes by and your pay envelope buys less and less, the problem of inflation further compromises your lifestyle.

Instead of noble words, there must be an all-out national effort to fight inflation, involving great sacrifices in the way you live. And, to be sure, Washington must keep a steady hand on the nation's delicate economic machinery in an effort to slow down the rate of price hikes and wage increases.

Economists feel, however, that even a major government-induced recession (dangerous because it could lead to a depression) won't cure the current rate of price increases. "The problem won't really be solved until people demand that government do something about it," sums up Kaufman.

No one is yet saying that a parallel exists with the Germany of the 1920's, when it took a bushel of marks to buy essential food items. But the seeds are there.

Since 1969, the cost of food, clothing, and other consumer items has rocketed 30%, and in some cases much more. Washington's response was a series of anti-inflation policies that produced wage and price controls and, in turn, economic shortages and dislocations in the marketplace that have left the United States reeling.

Federal Reserve Board Chairman Arthur Burns has labeled the situation a "Latin-American-type of inflation," which distorts the entire economy.

Many in Washington felt that Burns attempted to warn the Nixon Administration and the Congress—in sophisticated central bank language, so as not to scare anyone out of their pants—that unless a concerted effort is made to control inflation, a public loss of confidence in the ability of the government to run the country could shake the United States to its roots.

"It's hard to run an economy when no one has any faith that it is going to be around tomorrow," says Barry Bosworth, an economist with the Brookings Institution. "I don't agree with the gloom and doom prophets, but this year [1974] there is more logic to such fears."

What Bosworth and a number of other Americans in government, business, and academic life are watching more closely than inflation's erosion of the dollar, is inflation's destruction of confidence in the fabric of the capitalist system.

One of the believers in the confidence barometer is Frank Harrington, vice-president for corporate social responsibility at the Philadelphia-based INA Corporation, the financial services company.

"We're in an economic situation unparalleled in my lifetime," declares the 60-year-old Harrington. "There are unprecedented uncertainties."

For Harrington and INA, the uncertainties hit close to home. INA's business includes life insurance, and Harrington noted that some customers are borrowing on, or cashing in their policies and investing the proceeds into short-term, high-yielding instruments such as U.S. Treasury bills and bank certificates of deposit.

It's not a "1929-get-rich-quick-mentality" that's motivating the change in investment habits, says Harrington.

People simply want to build a nest egg for the future and they have come to question the economic institutions that once protected this nest egg.

* * *

Erosion of confidence. In a nutshell that's what has caused more Americans than ever before to shift their money out of traditional investments such as the stock market (a one-time surefire inflation hedge) and to consider alternatives to income out of relatively low-interest-paying bank and savings and loan accounts.

A lot of professional money has been opting for gold- and silver-related investments, foreign currency, and the like. It's high time the smaller investor—you—learned about the same options and how to use them.

If used prudently and wisely, these nontraditional (to Americans) forms of investment will help you make money during periods of high inflation by taking advantage of the economic conditions of the day. And since inflation is going to be around at a high level for longer than Washington is willing to acknowledge, you have plenty of time to hedge your income.

*   *   *

"Double-digit" is the key catch phrase in Washington to describe the inflation of our times. And there were no reassuring words in 1974 from our government leaders that solace was around the corner.

No less than John T. Dunlop, up to 1974 the director of President Nixon's Cost of Living Council, predicted that the United States will have a "persistent" inflation problem for the rest of this decade and into the next. Mr. Dunlop told Congress that, like a hamster on a treadmill, big wage and price boosts in the second half of 1974 will help neutralize the small progress the Administration had been making in battling inflation.

Most economists, bankers, and other inflation watchdogs, both in and out of government, agree with Dunlop's grim assessment.

Mr. Nixon dismantled his Cost of Living Council and the wage and price control machinery that accompanied it. But President Ford said he would revive a cost of living panel to act as a watchdog over the economy without going the full wage and price control route.

A survey by the American Statistical Association of Washington, D.C., and the National Bureau of Economic Research of New York, found that 62 economists, including some of the nation's leading professional forecasters, felt that inflation would get worse, not better.

Enforcing this view, Chase Econometrics, a division of Chase Manhattan Bank of New York, said in May of 1974 that "the inflation picture continues to be very gloomy ... we now expect double-digit inflation to continue throughout the rest of the year. The increase in the consumer price index is expected to average over 10% during the second half of the year, resulting in an 11% increase for the year as a whole."

Only one question really remains for the near term: Just how bad will it get?

*   *   *

Already the United States inflation rate exceeds that of many other countries.

In the past, Americans upset over steep rises in the inflation rate could at least get some comfort out of the fact that prices were going up faster almost everywhere else.

Before 1973, there was hardly a major country whose inflation rate didn't exceed that of the United States.

Today, seven countries in Western Europe and eleven in other parts of the world are experiencing more moderate inflation rates in their consumer prices. The International Monetary Fund provides the following information on our inflation rate compared to that of other nations. The first column shows 1973's inflation rate figures against the level of inflation for a period of time roughly covering 1972:

	1973	1972
United States	9.4%	4.7%
Austria	7.8%	7.6%
Belgium	7.5%	7.0%
France	8.4%	6.4%
West Germany	7.8%	6.9%
The Netherlands	8.2%	7.7%
Norway	8.5%	7.7%
Sweden	8.0%	6.0%

To be sure, two other major European industrialized countries—Great Britain and Italy—still have inflation rates that exceed the United States' rate, both recording increases of over 13% in 1973. Another industrial power, Japan, rang up a 20.4% inflation increase for the year.

Inflation is caused by the profligate ways of the government's fiscal and monetary policies.

Wasteful fiscal planning could be observed in recent years as the Nixon Administration proposed and Congress enacted one bloated federal budget after another with fat to be found in everything from record military spending to pork barrel financing of public works projects. Additionally, tax cuts at the wrong time had the impact of pumping too much money into the economy, and, in turn, increasing what was already a strong demand for goods and services.

On the monetary side, the Federal Reserve Board, by manipulating the nation's money and credit supplies, has control over the amount of cash channeled through the economy to the public.

But those who run this complex economic machinery have historically tended to be moved by public pressure rather than good economic sense. Washington's politicians would not risk a rise in the sensitive unemployment index, preferring to give consumers more money to spend rather than vote for austerity.

Unfortunately inflation feeds upon itself.

Unions ask for big wage increases so that workers can keep up with rising prices. The spiral continues as goods and services become more expensive because there are more dollars chasing them. The treadmill is seemingly endless. And just when we seemed to be making progress in 1971, everything appeared to go haywire.

In early 1971, the Federal Reserve was slowing the rate of inflation by permitting only moderate growth of the money supply. But in August of that year, President Nixon caved in to political pressures and imposed wage and price controls, which were then followed by a fresh round of fiscal and monetary stimulants, and then by an acceleration of inflation in 1973 when controls were relaxed.

* * *

Atop the mechanics of inflation is the psychology of the sickness. It can be summed up in two words: "Inflationary Expectations." This is what people *think* is going to happen to wages and prices. It governs what labor unions will ask for in their contracts as well as how businesses plan production schedules for the year. Pressure for higher interest rates builds when lenders see sharply rising prices stimulating the demand for money. They try to protect themselves by insisting on higher rates. Thus, 1974 saw the highest interest rates in this country's history.

The problem has been a long time developing and is so entrenched that it will be a way of life for a long time to come. Since the end of World War II, the government has preferred to push for maximum employment, production, and purchasing power. This was much more palatable to politicians than risking a transition period from a wartime to a peacetime economy that might sink into a depression reminiscent of the 1930's.

Today you are paying the price for this policy. The erosion of the purchasing power of the dollar, in fact, has replaced crime as the citizen's number-one concern.

Arthur E. Sindlinger, the founder of Sindlinger's Economic Service, developed a consumer confidence survey which reaches up to 2,000 households a week by telephone. He says consumers are desperate.

In an interview with Robert J. Donovan, associate editor of the Los Angeles *Times,* Sindlinger said:

"Here is the fundamental fact: From 1957 through 1972, three-fourths of the nation every week were gaining in their . . . affluence. Now only one-fourth of the nation is gaining. One-half are standing still, and one-fourth are losing ground because prices keep rising and their income can't keep pace. You can't have anything but a recession with that situation."

"All through the years from 1957 to May of 1971," says Sindlinger, "almost everybody liked inflation. In 1957, the median income of all households was less than $5,500 a year. By May, 1971, it had risen to almost $13,000—quite a jump."

Sputnik, the Cold War, Vietnam—all were responsible for the United States flexing its economic muscles during the period discussed by Sindlinger. "Almost every household in the country was making progress during that period," notes Sindlinger. "Up to May, 1971, everybody liked inflation."

But then the machinery began breaking down, partly under the weight of large new wage contracts. Prices began to outstrip income, and inflation was finally shown to be the disease it really is.

* * *

Where it obviously comes home to roost is in that deteriorating dollar in your pocket. And who gets hurt the most? Why the little guy, of course!

INFLATION AND INVESTMENT, AN INTRODUCTION

The fellow who salts away a little every payday in a bank or savings and loan association is being ripped off much more than the wealthy who can afford more sophisticated and expensive forms of investment (as we shall discuss later). For example, a United States savings bond purchased for $75 in 1966 is now worth only $73.17, despite the accumulation of $26.68 in interest—when inflation is taken into account.

An average factory worker who earned $123 a week in take-home pay in 1972, and got the 5.5% raise allowed by federal guidelines in 1973, actually suffered a loss of $4.06 in purchasing power.

For those living on fixed pensions, the situation is even more desperate. Congress has increased Social Security benefits religiously (and, incidentally, taken more money out of workers' paychecks through higher Social Security taxes, which hit the lower-paid workers the hardest), but an elderly person who depends upon Social Security to survive is worse off now than in 1965 because of the unrelenting erosion of his or her purchasing power.

If you retire on a pension of $12,000 a year but face an increase in living costs of 6% annually (which has suddenly become an almost "acceptable" rate of inflation, a sick commentary on the times) during the next decade, you would need $21,500 to live as well in 1984, or an increase of $9,500.

There are the alarmists—or pragmatists, if you will—who are expecting better than a 9% inflation rate for the next ten years. If they are right you will then need $28,-404 to live as well in 1984 as you can live on $12,000 in 1974.

HERE IS WHAT IT HAS TAKEN TO STAY
EVEN AT TWO INCOME LEVELS*
(FAMILY OF FOUR)

	1967	1973	% Of Increase
Total Budget	**$5,915**	**$8,181**	**38%**
Food	1,644	2,440	48
Housing	1,303	1,627	25
Transportation	446	563	26
Clothing and personal care	700	901	29
Medical care	474	660	39
Other	610	774	27
Income taxes	738	1,216	65
Social Security	265	492	86
Federal and state taxes	473	724	55
Total Budget	**$13,050**	**$18,201**	**40%**
Food	2,586	4,020	55
Housing	3,340	4,386	31
Transportation	1,127	1,315	17
Clothing and personal care	1,446	1,846	28
Medical	497	692	39
Other	1,782	2,215	24
Income taxes	2,272	3,727	64
Social Security	303	647	113.5
Federal and state taxes	1,969	3,080	57

Source: Conference Board, based on government statistics.

Helping you protect against the erosion of your savings is the objective of this book. It is built upon the premise that high inflation is here to stay for at least the near term; that is, the inflation level will remain near double-digit or higher during this decade.

Otto E. Roethenmund, vice-chairman of the board of directors of the Foreign Commerce Bank of Zurich, Switzerland, and one of the world's more astute inflation-watchers, agrees. For the time being, the United States will have to live with it. He says he's "only afraid that accelerated inflation can lead to runaway inflation, and runaway inflation will be the end of the present type of United States economy. Runaway inflation can only end in disaster, meaning a major depression."

By no means do I applaud the doomsday advocates. Those who say that paper money is completely worthless unless entirely backed by gold, or who see the inevitable collapse of the United States economy and worldwide economic chaos, are only fooling themselves and playing on the fears of the ignorant.

The United States dollar still remains one of the cornerstones of international exchange, whether it is backed by gold or goat's hair. What stands behind the dollar is the full faith and integrity of the world's most powerful nation. If *that* is destroyed, then, indeed, the dollar won't be worth the specially treated paper it's printed on.

But the United States is not at an advanced stage of decay, and it doesn't yet make sense to run out and build a retreat in your favorite mountain range.

The problem is a matter of degree. One thing is certain: the dollar's purchasing power has been diminished. And that is the reason for this book: to give the investor some alternatives—tools to neutralize that erosion. I simply want you to know how to hedge against inflation.

"The worst thing you could do is leave your money in the bank." That is the opinion of James Sinclair, an international monetary expert with the Wall Street house of Vilas & Hickey. Sinclair says, "If the interest you are receiving is not equal to the consumer price index, then please tell me what good is the whole thing?" He's right.

Now I am not advocating that you pull *all* of your money out of your bank or savings account and put it into gold coins and the like.

However, I *am* going to outline a strategy for Defensive Investing.

This is a book for the majority of Americans who will prudently keep a portion of their savings in the bank, but who at the same time have decided to protect their years of labor against dollar-consuming inflation.

If some of the recommendations seem far-fetched, it may just be that you have never ventured further than the stock market. Remember that the rate of inflation we are experiencing and which lies ahead is unprecedented in the American experience. Therefore, it is not a radical statement to say that depending on the inflation rate, 50% or more of your savings should be working for you in investment outside of a bank or savings and loan.

There are, of course, risks with all investments. Nothing recommended in this book is guaranteed to make a fortune overnight. But it's the author's objective to offer some alternatives to the reader on how to make money work during the high inflation times of the present and the possible hyper-inflation times of the future.

* * *

Pollster Sindlinger's mid-1974 consumer attitude testing showed that 85% of all Americans expect prices to go higher before peaking.

But relatively few Americans know what anti-inflation tools are available to them—tools that, in the past, have been the devices of the sophisticated money manager who naturally turns to what he feels are inflation-sheltered investments during times of economic instability.

The Inflation Game's rules are relatively easy to digest. And anyone can play.

Chapter II

KEEPING UP WITH
THE JONESES

—*Bonds and Short-Term*
Money Market Instruments

Pity the poor housewife—Japanese housewife, that is. Skyrocketing world food costs boosted the price of a pound of boneless sirloin steak to $14.70 in Tokyo in May of 1974, a record even for inflation-riddled Japan. That was a $4.39 leap over March. Yet that sort of knowledge doesn't take the sting out of the fact that the United States is gradually gaining full membership in the Hyperinflation Club as the American housewife will attest to with an increasingly strident voice.

Sirloin in Washington, D.C., for example, during those same two months rose from $2.29 to $2.59 a pound, about 20 cents higher than the price of the same cut in Paris.

Soaring food prices are only one example—albeit a glaring one—of how inflation is taking an increasingly larger chunk out of your paycheck. Keeping up with the Joneses is no longer the goal of many Americans simply because the proverbial Joneses are sinking in the same quagmire of eroded income.

The name of the game now is simply keeping afloat.

Never in our nation's history has the economic climate been as muddled as it is today. People making as much as $50,000 or $60,000 a year have extended themselves to the point where they are pleading with creditors for extra time to pay their bills. By the time the typical family has paid for the bare essentials—food, housing, utilities, medical care—there's hardly enough left to pay another installment on the car or to meet the monthly credit card bills.

The American Bankers Association says its figures on tardy installment payments are the highest since it began collecting such information 20 years ago.

Inflation—that cruelest tax of all—is eating away at income and savings at a double-digit clip so we must devise new ways to protect our income and standard of living. Granted, Washington may cut the rate of inflationary wage and price increases that keep us in the hole, but "the new poor"—America's vast middle class—is going to have to adjust it's traditional way of thinking on how to make money work.

Expanding international economies have brought tremendous advances in the way we can enjoy our lives. But with expansion has come a persistently high level of worldwide inflation that isn't disastrous if we can adjust our habits and pay the high price of a world growing smaller and more interrelated.

First, stop being bitter over rising prices. You're probably not rolling with the punch in a new milieu that demands new saving and investing techniques. As you'll see, it's certainly not too late to adjust.

If you've talked to the Joneses lately, you'll probably discover that your next-door neighbors aren't counting on the stock market anymore as a hedge against inflation. And if you look in your stock portfolio you'll quickly see why.

If you put $1.000 into some typical common stocks five years ago, the market value now is approximately $845. With $190 in dividends this brings the value of your investment to $1,035. But the 32% increase in living costs since mid-1969—the so-called inflation tax—has turned your gain into a real loss of over $200.

Common stocks still appear to be a good inflation hedge over *the long run* (investors who hung on to their shares a decade or more made money even if they bought stocks at or near the bull market highs of 1882, 1907, 1929, or 1936). But most individuals who snapped up stocks on the market uptick of the mid-1960's still haven't achieved significant gains.

According to Interactive Data Corporation, the average stock price decline on the Big Board in 1973 was 26.4%. Additionally, 599 of the 1,481 issues lost 40% or more of their value.

Stocks on the American Stock Exchange fared even

worse, suffering an average drop of 39.8%; 695 of the 1,155 issues plunged 40% or more.

Moreover, at this writing, the broad-based indicators such as the New York Stock Exchange common stock index and Standard & Poor's 500- and 425-stock compilations were sitting on their 1974 lows. This was in the face of Wall Street research reports documenting that the Big Board's 1,500 issues had slipped, on average, below their 1962 bottom.

The rationale that corporate profits can be expected to rise along with prices, thus allowing dividends to keep up with inflation, simply isn't working. Under this archaic theory, as dividends rise, the market price of common stocks will also tend to rise.

Stocks .then, are no longer insurance against modern-day inflation.

Then there is "stagflation."

Now part of our language of the seventies, stagflation refers to a high rate of inflation while at the same time Washington is attempting to use fiscal (spending and taxing) and monetary (money supply and credit) policies to slow down the economy. Unfortunately for you and me, we get the worst of both.

The roots of this dilemma appeared after the Vietnam War. Inflation overtook the U.S. economy in 1965, and monetary policy was tightened. The subsequent business recession caused stocks to drop sharply in 1969 and 1970, chasing many small investors away from the stock market and knocking the market for a 15% bearish loop.

For the few who stayed through the 1971 market recovery, they found themselves in the same stagflation bind as the value of corporate stockholdings declined to the tune of $193 billion.

Putting your money back into the bank or your neighborhood savings and loan association isn't going to help matters either. Earning 5.25% (set by Federal law) on a passbook savings account just may be the worst sin you can commit during a high inflation period. To be sure, you should have a cushion in your nearby bank or savings and loan to see you meet day-to-day bills and any unforeseen calamities. You should have at least two to six months' salary in a passbook account, advise many bankers and economists. But it's high time you looked at bonds and, more importantly, short-term money market instruments, a mouthful that's likely to scare away the average person before it's understood that these may be the most sensible ways of defensive investing.

Only a few years ago, bonds were scoffed at by profit-minded investors as a conservative hedge for the weaker-spirited among us. But inflation and a plunging stock market changed all that.

A University of Chicago computer study showed that the total return (dividends and appreciation) from stocks for the period January, 1926, through December, 1965, was 9.3%. Quality bonds (rated by Standard & Poor's and Moody's) are providing almost as much these days—around 8%—and the risk is vastly reduced.

With a bond you're not going to be subject to erratic price swings and the possibility of a missed dividend (sorry about that, Con Ed!). The corporation issuing the bond has a contract to pay you a specific interest rate until your principal is returned on a specific date. Should you decide to sell the bond before it matures, you might lose a little on what you paid for it, but the 8% yield you've enjoyed in the meantime should more than soothe your inflation-jangled nerves. Also, a bondholder is a debtor who is one of the first in line if a company goes under. A shareholder, on the other hand, stands to lose everything.

Short of another Penn Central type of catastrophe, with your portfolio comfortably lined with quality bonds, there's no need to nervously turn to the stock market tables every morning. And bonds can be purchased on more liberal margin (down payment) terms than stock.

As in everything else I am going to discuss, set your sights high and shoot for quality in bonds. Naturally, the yield may be lower, but this is more than compensated for by knowing the risk also is minimal.

Standard & Poor's and Moody's assign 12 different ratings to corporate bonds, ranging from triple-A to single-D, based on the firm's ability to repay its loans. Wall Streeters know that they are entering speculative territory when they start dipping into the "B's" and although the yield might be noticeably higher—1% or more—the ratio of risk probably doesn't make it worthwhile for the average investor who can't analyze a company prospectus with the same experienced eye as a bank, insurance company, or mutual fund.

An 8% yield to maturity may turn out to be attractive, for example, if the level of inflation can be reduced to a 7% annual rate or less by the end of 1974. Thus, such a yield would keep the bond investor barely ahead of the inflation rate. The 8.8% coupon on the triple-A rated $500 million batch of American Telephone & Telegraph bonds offered in May of 1974 had just such an appeal and was snapped up by investors looking for a solid better-than-passbook return for their excess cash. Even better, a June, 1974, Pacific Telephone offering carried a record (for Ma Bell) 9.59% coupon, and again was quickly sold out.

It's best not to do anything exotic in the bond market. After all, you're not out for an overnight fortune but, hopefully, for steady intermediate or long-term gains. Keep in mind that bond prices are directly impacted by interest rates. If you decide to sell a $1,000 bond with 5% or 6% yield you might run into trouble unloading if current rates are around 8% to 9%. That's where you could take that minor loss we were talking about on the principal.

Moreover, since it is usually a little harder to sell bonds, stay with issues listed on the New York Stock Exchange and away from speculative issues. And be sure to check the bond's call protection. A company forced by soaring interest rates to offer a 9% coupon may have the option of recalling the bond when interest rates drop. Utilities, for example, try to achieve five-year call protection against fluctuating interest rates. Industrials generally seek ten-year protection.

You should also be aware that there is a growing feeling that the bond market is not the traditional haven for investors that it once was. More and more, Wall Street analysts point out, the stock and bond markets go down together.

Those new to the bond market found in the spring of

[25]

1974 that utility bonds issued in February at par ($1,000 per bond) offering yields of nearly 9% dropped in value as interest rates climbed. In May, these bonds were selling for around $920.

Certainly, an investor could say he buys bonds to hold to maturity, and with a 9% return what difference does a "paper loss" make? But what if an emergency arises and you have to sell the bond before maturity?

Take that by now infamous Consolidated Edison situation. When Con Ed passed its second quarter dividend in April of 1974, its bonds plunged in value and its rating dropped.

Seek out the advice of a reputable broker on questions of whether to buy old or new bonds and other subtleties of the bond market. Or, if all of this still boggles the mind, if you have trouble computing principal and yield and, like stocks, have had little luck in the selection process, a bond fund might be more your cup of tea.

Bond funds have proliferated, especially in the past few years, against the background of rising interest rates. You may have to pay a fee of 8% or so for this kind of expertise plus an annual management fee, but in return you'll have a piece of a bond portfolio that is far more diversified than the average individual could afford. This is in addition to the price advantages that the individual can't get because of the large positions the funds can take.

Do some checking into funds, however, before you leap. Some, for all of their expertise, may be riskier than they look. One recent study showed that some tax-exempt bond funds, which provide tax-sheltered income from the interest on bonds issued by state and local municipalities (a $3 billion business), were overextending themselves. In an attempt to show performance through high yield, the fund managers were purchasing low-grade issues with below-average marketability and above-average risk of default.

Most mutual funds, however, make an honest professional effort to provide the investor with the expertise not generally available to the public and, hopefully, funnel greater returns than a person would have received managing his own stock and/or bond portfolio. The trouble is that like the stock market, mutual funds—a reflection of the market—have recently left a lot to be desired.

The 180 funds in Barron's Quarterly Mutual Fund Record suffered an average per share loss of 19.8% in the last quarter of 1973 against a 17.2% loss for the Dow Jones Composite Average. Investors were clearly frightened. Individuals cashed in $5.7 billion of mutual fund shares in 1973, while buying only $4.4 billion worth.

But a few funds were gold mines—literally—because the bulk of their assets was invested in gold mining stocks. International Investors was one such fund, posting an astounding 88.6% per share increase in 1973. We shall discuss the gold funds in a later chapter.

Another type of mutual fund has shown sharp gains—due primarily to inflation-caused high interest rates. And here is one area where you, the small investor, stand to benefit from inflation the same way the big boys—the professional money managers with the nation's major financial institutions—do their investing.

These funds invest in what's known as short-term money market instruments. This is financial jargon for

Treasury bills and other government notes, bank certificates of deposit, and corporate commercial paper. If you want maximum short-term gain, particularly if you are a pensioner living on a fixed income, they may be just what you are looking for.

Rates on these instruments zoomed to the neighborhood of 11% in 1973 and through the first half of 1974.

And with at least two of these instruments—Treasury bills and certificates of deposit—there's more safety than in stocks and bonds. Treasury bills have the full faith and credit of the United States. Most certificates of deposit have at least some Federal government insurance behind them.

This is certainly a lot more attractive situation than letting the money wilt away in a passbook savings account or watching it disappear in the stock market.

The catch used to be that you needed $100,000 to benefit from the high interest rate of a bank certificate of deposit or commercial paper or $10,000 to buy a Treasury bill. Moreover, the management of these types of investments, which may come due every few months, is a time-consuming task, requiring no little degree of financial skill to keep reinvesting them (otherwise known as "rolling them over").

Several new mutual funds circumvent these problems. They specialize in these instruments and have done remarkably well with investors' money amid rocketing interest rates. Therefore, these funds are a natural inflation hedge. Among them are:

—Reserve Fund, 1301 Avenue of the Americas, New York, N.Y. 10019.

—Money Market Management Inc., 421 Seventh Avenue, Pittsburgh, Pa. 15219.

—Dreyfus Liquid Assets, Inc., 600 Madison Avenue, New York, N.Y. 10022.

The Reserve Fund was organized by the New York firm of Brown & Bent, a small investment house. It began selling U.S. government obligations and certificates of deposit—but not commercial paper. In January of 1973, Brown & Bent had $400,000 in these instruments. By mid-1974. it had run this total to $180 million.

In the opinion of Bruce Bent, one of the fund's directors, commercial paper was too great a risk. "We would not expose investors to it." With government obligations, Washington stands behind them, he added. Most major banks which issue certificates of deposit, of course, are supervised by the Federal Reserve Board. But, observed Bent, who's supervising the corporations that issue commercial paper?

Bent said that about one-third of the Reserve Fund's assets come from investors disenchanted with the stock market. And, make no mistake about it, corporations and institutions know how to play the interest rate game too. That's where Bent and the other short-term money managers get a lot of their operating cash.

To some extent, what Bent says is true about commercial paper, in effect short-term corporate IOU's. This has traditionally been a financing channel for corporations who wish to put idle cash to work. Billions of dollars in commercial paper changes hands daily. There is currently over $50 billion outstanding.

Of all of the major short-term money market instruments, corporate commercial paper is likely to have the highest yield because, as Bent says, it has the highest risk—it is a direct *unsecured* obligation of a firm, in many cases a finance company. Commercial paper maturities range from five to 270 days with the quality of the paper rated by Moody's and Standard & Poor's.

As you can see, the yield of commercial paper *has* to be higher than the other instruments. There is no federal agency that has the responsibility to back commercial paper instruments and there is no Securities & Exchange Commission that will act as a watchdog to insure their quality. The usual individual minimum investment is $100,000, although Merrill Lynch Government Securities Inc., a subsidiary of the world's largest brokerage house, offers some top-rated commercial paper in $25,000 denominations for a $25 fee.

A few companies, such as General Motors Acceptance Corporation and Chrysler Financial Corporation, offer their commercial paper directly to the public with lower interest rates but lower minimum purchase requirements, too.

Charles Bradburn of Money Market Management tends to refute the criticism of commercial paper as an investment. He says it is safe to invest part of your cash into commercial paper—but only that with the highest quality rating from Moody's or Standard & Poor's. Bradburn's fund, which started in January of 1974, built its assets to

$17 million in three months on the investment of 2,650 shareholders.

Another new short-term fund is Dreyfus Liquid Assets. Saul Smerling, one of the fund's officials, said there's no doubt that popularity of the fund, which had $40 million in assets by mid-1974, is clearly due to hyperinflation. Smerling said the reason for commercial paper's success is the higher interest rates offered by these instruments and the wide play in the press and financial publications. "My gut feeling is that we're getting sophisticated investors, but there's also widespread interest from the small investor," said Smerling. He added that interest rates would have to come down to the savings and loan passbook level before some of the glitter of the short-terms would begin to tarnish.

Actually, except for subtle differences the operations of these three funds are practically identical. They are no-load investment companies because there is no sales charge or redemption fee. The only cost is a one-half percentage point management fee and a fee for fund expenses up to another one-half point.

As explained by Money Market Management's Bradburn: "If you invest $1,000 which earns 10%, we take one-half of 1% of the 10%—or $5—for the management fee and then another one-half of 1% for the expenses of running the fund, such as printing prospectuses. This comes to $10. So out of the $100 yield, the shareholder gets a $90 return."

Perhaps the most important difference is in the minimum amount an investor must initially kick in. The Reserve Fund's minimum was $1,000, and additional investments had to be in $1,000 lots. Money Market Management also began business at the $1,000 level, but at this printing required a minimum initial investment of $5,000; but additional chunks could be added in $100 amounts. Dreyfus required an investment of at least $5,000 with $1,000 additional amounts.

If your appetite for this type of investment is whetted. consider this: customers of the Reserve Fund earned 7.66% on their money, net of all expenses and fees, in 1973.

Money Market Management says it was able to pay shareholders 8.4% net, after deducting the fund's expenses. Dreyfus paid a similar rate of return to its investors. And for some periods all three funds, reflecting record interest levels, were returning above 9%.

(The hardnosed among us may look across the Atlantic and see where our British cousins snapped up nearly a billion dollars worth of their government's gilt-edged securities at a record 12¾% in 1974. But don't forget, Great Britain's rate of inflation still dwarfs what Americans are experiencing, thus making Uncle Sam's securities highly competitive.)

If you are more of the do-it-yourself rugged individualist, here's some information you ought to have handy before you plunge into the short-terms.

U.S. Treasury bills have enjoyed the greatest popularity with the short-term investor. The Federal Reserve auctions the bills weekly and monthly, the former with maturities of three or six months which are available at the 36 Federal banks and branches, the latter having 12-month maturity dates. And don't forget, if you have the

$10,000 required initial outlay, you can buy in multiples of $5,000 after that.

Parenthetically, the potential for a massive switch into T-bills by the public obviously worried the government to the point where Washington, under pressure from the savings and loans and the home building industry, has raised the minimum denomination from $1,000 to $10,000.

"There's no escaping it," said a Treasury official. "Some people have got to get screwed. The trick is to find the policies that will prevent the burden from falling too heavily on one group or another."

By the time this book is in circulation, however, Congress may have restored the $1,000 denomination. Many influential Congressmen got mad over the Treasury decision, arguing that the small saver should be able to obtain interest rates as high as those offered the big investor.

You can get forms to buy Treasury bills at or by writing a letter to your nearest Federal Reserve Bank (your local banker has the address) and describing the issue you want and the amount you want to pay. Don't forget to enclose a certified check or a bank draft made payable to the Federal Reserve Bank. (The weekly auction of bills is on Mondays, unless there's a holiday, in which case it would be on the preceding Friday. Your letter must be postmarked no later than the Sunday before the Monday auction).

If you want to bid against the big institutions, just submit your written bid stating what you're willing to pay for the bills. If you bid lower than what the Treasury will accept, you'll end up with nothing but your check back in the mail. At one auction in March of 1974, the Treasury received bids on three-month bills totaling $5.2 billion, but accepted only about half that amount at prices yielding 7.900% to 7.932%.

If you're buying under $200,000 in Treasury bills, you don't have to compete for the securities. Submit what's known as a noncompetitive tender, simply an agreement to pay the average price of all the bids that come to the Treasury on that particular issue.

What you'll receive from the government is a "discount check." This represents the difference between the actual purchase and the face value. This is equivalent to your interest or yield, and as a noncompetitive purchaser you accept the results of the bids submitted by the big institutional investors.

Let's say you want $10,000 worth of three- or six-month T-bills. You write a check for $10,000 and give the check to the Federal Reserve. On Thursday, the third day after the auction, the Federal Reserve sends you a check for the amount of the discount. If the yield is 8%, you would receive a check for $200. Because this return is earned on only $9,800, your actual coupon equivalent yield is somewhat higher. Then, at maturity, the investor has a choice of cashing in the face value of the bill or "rolling them over" and using the proceeds to buy more bills.

(The $200 discount is figured by computing the interest on a 360-day basis so that you have a *per diem* interest rate. Then multiply the *per diem* rate by the number of days you are holding the Treasury bill. Finally, subtract this amount from the par value of the bill.)

If you go through an intermediary such as a broker or

a bank, there may be a charge for handling this sort of transaction, which should come to $10 or $20 on a $10,-000 investment.

And then there are the Treasury notes and bonds which are not sold at a discount but instead bear a specified rate of interest. Treasury bills come only in bearer (negotiable) form, but bonds and notes can come either in the bearer form or registered in an individual's name. Note and bond offerings are not held on specific dates but rather are announced a few weeks before the date of issue.

If you purchase bearer bonds, guard them carefully or lock them in your safety deposit box, because anyone can cash them. Several major federal agency obligations come in this form.

Incidentally, if you don't have $10,000 to invest in Treasury bills with their 8% interest, take a look at these Treasury notes and bonds which have somewhat higher yields but longer maturity dates and which may be purchased in smaller denominations.

The highest rates are in the Federal agency issues where minimum denominations range from $1,000 to $1 million (for institutional customers, obviously) and where the interest yield runs from about 6.5% to above 9%.

The agency market is divided into two groups. The federally sponsored group includes the 12 Federal Home Loan Banks which together form, in effect, the "central bank" for the savings and loan industry; the Banks for Cooperatives; the Federal Intermediate Credit Banks; the Federal Land Banks; the Federal National Mortgage Association (Fanny Mae); and the Government National Mortgage Association (Ginny Mae).

The second group consists of government guaranteed agencies. From this category you get securities issued by the Export-Import Bank, the Federal Housing Administration, the U.S. Postal Service, and others.

There are some good reasons why you should divert some of your savings into these obligations, aside from the obvious fact that you are going to receive a much higher interest rate than you can get from the banks and savings and loans.

First (unlike some other investments we shall explore), there is a great deal of liquidity in the agency markets. This means that you don't have to worry about selling your holdings. If you want to cash them in before maturity, the huge turnover in Treasury and agency securities by corporations and institutions readily puts buyers and sellers together in the busy secondary market for these issues. Secondly, the transaction fee is either very low or, in the case of agency bonds, nonexistent. And, in all cases, you can sleep contentedly at night with the knowledge that short of a White House coup your securities are backed by the highest credit rating you can find, thus guaranteeing payment of interest and principal.

(This situation is creating big problems for the savings and loans. The financial disease afflicting these institutions during times of high inflation is known as "disintermediation"—that is, savers are pulling huge chunks of their savings out of savings and loans and funneling them into the higher government yields. And since the savings and loan industry was established as the financing backbone of our housing industry, any big shift in deposits has an immediate effect in the mortgage market. In 1974, mortgage money sources dried up to a point where federal regulators may have to overhaul the entire structure of home financing.)

Your friendly broker or banker may not always be the easiest to deal with when you want to buy government securities. The commissions on these instruments are tiny. Dealers say it is a headache dealing with the small or "odd" lot sought by the individual investor. Obviously, they want the bigger commissions of the institutions. If you experience any difficulty, write the government agency in which you are interested, inquire whether you can buy direct or whether you would be better off going through a dealer, and, with a self-addressed envelope, tell the agency you want the location of the nearest convenient outlet. Your tax dollars are paying the salaries of these bureaucrats! Hopefully, they'll respond.

Some of the government agency issues have indeed been a mystery investment to the public at large but may be worth your time investigating. Take Ginny Mae (Government National Mortgage Association), for example.

When Ginny Mae first appeared in 1970, the minimum unit you could purchase from brokers was $100,000. Then the minimum unit was cut to $25,000, which allowed a number of individuals to join that exclusive club which counts insurance companies and pension funds among its membership. And in 1973 the Minnesota Housing and Finance Agency brought out a $30 million offering of these mortgage-backed securities in $5,000 units. What's more, Ginny Mae yields which can run 8% and up are exempt from Federal income tax.

Ginny Mae had its roots in the credit crunch of

1969-70 when mortgage money began drying up as fast as it did in 1974. Under the legislation passed by Congress, Ginny Mae was established to allow savings and loans, banks, and other mortgage lenders to pool their mortgages, issue certificates on them, and sell them to the public. It made more housing money available and the government guaranteed the mortgage money pool. Over $10 billion worth of Ginny Mae securities were sold through 1974. And you can buy Ginny Mae notes through your broker.

Ginny Mae issues have a distinct advantage over the average corporate bond, too. Not only are they "backed by the full faith and credit of the United States Government," Ginny Mae certificates generally assure the investor that the high yield will be there for about 12 years. Thus, you won't lose a high interest return if rates suddenly drop. (Remember—corporate and utility bonds may have a call-back feature.)

Furthermore, with Ginny Mae you have diversified into real estate, which, as we shall see in another section of this book, is a pretty good idea during high inflation times; and you've done it without the accompanying headache of collecting rent and the rest of the bookkeeping complexities of owning property. Finally, as is the case with other government securities, the secondary market in Ginny Maes is healthy so that if you want to sell before maturity, any one of a number of brokerage houses will buy them back for only a slight fee of, say, $100 on a $25,000 certificate.

This vignette of Ginny Mae is just one example of the opportunity for the investor who takes a little time to investigate what the government offers in the way of high-yielding safe securities.

Rubbing shoulders with the fat cat institutions is more difficult when you seek to reap windfall yields on bank certificates of deposit. Negotiable certificates of deposit issued by the nation's major commercial banks are ordinarily available to anyone with $100,000 or more to invest. Many of the largest banks, however, prefer to deal only in $1 million lots. Maturities on these certificates range from 30 days to over a year, and were yielding over 8% in the 1974 secondary market.

Bankers acceptances also are offered by commercial banks. This originally was a draft drawn on a bank, usually by an exporter or importer, with a maturity date corresponding to the delivery of the goods being financed. The commercial bank sells such issues either to individual customers or to companies that make markets in these instruments. The original concept of bankers acceptances was simply to finance international trade. Today, however, this has been greatly expanded and banks use a variety of kinds of loans as the basis for acceptances. You can buy these instruments either through your bank or a dealer, and, like Treasury bills, they are sold at a discount and redeemed at face value. The smallest denomination is $25,000, but six-figure acceptances are more common. Maturities range up to 180 days with 1974 interest rates yielding over 8%.

In a nutshell . . .

Diversify your savings into government securities. The

risk is minimal and the interest return will keep you relatively close to today's inflation pace.

Avoid fees, if possible, because they reduce your yield. Treasury bills, for example, can be purchased directly from the Federal Reserve Bank. Likewise, they can be redeemed at the Federal Reserve.

Stay with high quality. That means buying U.S. government securities and certificates of deposit from only the largest commercial banks and—if the high yield is simply irresistible—despite the risk—purchasing only the highest-rated commercial paper.

Or for a fee, if you don't want to be bothered with individual management, the short-term money funds mentioned here say they can capably manage your cash and return high yields. So far, they've been right. There's complete liquidity—that is, if you need your money back in a hurry, it's there in a day or so. And you don't have to shell out as much cash to take advantage of the market which is being analyzed by professionals who probably can do a much better investing job than you, day in and day out.

What is a good rule of thumb for the short-term funds? The people who run these funds say cash in excess of current needs should be invested in this way. This would generally be cash you are leaving in a checking or savings and loan account.

Major pitfall:
If you decide to take on the short-term money market yourself you will have to keep steady track of the maturi-

ties of the issues in which you invest if you want to stay reinvested. This means "rolling over" or reinvesting the issues every few months when they come due. Obviously, this takes time and a continuing surveillance of the market. Moreover, sudden market fluctuations, especially downward, can leave you in a quandary over how to reinvest an instrument that was drawing 8% when you suddenly discover the market is calling for only 7% on that instrument. For the do-it-yourselfer, the best bet is to consult with your banker or broker.

Even if 7% inflation is achieved by the government in the near term—a difficult chore, at best—the short-term market is still one of the best hedges against erosion of the dollar's purchasing power. It's a solid way to diversify your portfolio with a minimum of risk. There's little chance that inflation will be reduced in the near term to the point where the strengths of the short-term market will be weakened.

You can tell the Joneses you have found a way to keep up with the two-digit increases in consumer prices without the risk of going over the deep end by taking a flyer on soybeans or risking a bundle on an as yet unheard of $1-a-share "sure thing."

But wait a minute, say your enterprising neighbors. There's a fixed dollar investment that wasn't mentioned that is sure to stay ahead of the inflation rat(e) race.

You can make a fortune overnight in real estate.

Chapter III

THE LAND BOOM
—Real Estate Investment

Many of America's so-called "new rich"—those who have amassed fortunes in this century, especially in the past few decades—have basically made their bundle in three fields: oil, insurance, and real estate. Through a combination of special tax breaks and subsidies, astute investors have literally been able to pyramid a few dollars into millions. Of these three areas, real estate is the one many feel is still open to the little guy who wants to take advantage of high inflation.

Chicago industrialist Marshall Field once said, "Buying real estate is not only the best way, the quickest way, and the safest way, but the only way to become wealthy."

The popularity of real estate investment can be measured in the fact that more money is invested in real estate than stocks and bonds. And land—the right land—has been leaping in value in recent years.

But one must make certain assumptions when investing in real estate. If you conclude that the world is heading for an inflation catastrophe involving international chaos and riots in the streets, then no dollar-denominated investment—including real estate, stocks, bonds, or savings accounts—will be worth the paper upon which the currency is printed. Even the school of moderate inflation argues against real estate, claiming there are liquidity problems—that is, you can't unload a piece of land or a building in time to avoid the crash and take your profit.

On the other hand, if you feel the world has enough sensible leaders to muddle their way through a period of high inflation with economic dislocations that don't signal the end of the world, then real estate deserves a serious look.

You might want to note that history has shown us that the world adjusts to hard times, whether economic or political. The years ahead will time and again produce surprise catastrophes which will ravage lands and kill tens of thousands. Governments will fall; economies will crumble. The so-called wise among us will caution that there are unprecedented situations creeping upon us that could destroy a lifetime of saving and reduce us to beggars on the streets.

The other school says it's a waste of time, effort, and cash to build bomb shelters and retreats. Two World Wars and a worldwide depression in this century already have taught us that like the ocean's tides, the good times and bad times are cyclical. Therefore, many a smart investor hangs on to a blue chip—whether it's stock or a piece of land—during bad times. In the long run, the reasoned odds tell us that unless the world ceases to function, such investments tend to rise in value.

Short of complete confiscation of property by our government, the takeover by a foreign power, or the utter collapse of society as we know it, real estate is an extremely solid investment. And if you have any further doubts, talk to a family that just sold their home at an astounding increase in value over the purchase price!

"Throughout the viable areas of the United States," observed Forest E. Olson, one of the nation's most successful real estate men, "property values have gone up from 20% to 50%" during the current wave of inflation.

"The costs of construction are going much higher," says Olson, "and higher labor demands plus materials shortages will contribute to the situation." Olson is Senior Vice-President with the Los Angeles-based Coldwell Banker, the largest independently owned real estate firm in the United States. This New York Stock Exchange-listed company does nearly $2 billion a year in industrial, commercial, and residential real estate, with offices in California, Texas, Arizona, Oregon, Washington, Colorado, and Georgia, and real estate connections all over the country.

The Chicago-based National Association of Realtors reports that an existing single-family home in 1966 had a median sales price of $18,760. In 1973, this had shot up to $28,920. In 1963, the median price for a new home was $22,200. Again, by 1973 this price had rocketed to $35,600.

Choice land and the structures on them are being sold

practically overnight, realtors across the United States report.

A liquidity problem? Only if your property is far out from an urban area, says Olson, *so* far out that its value is impacted. "A land's value is related to its utility," Olson explains, and the utility is many times related to its accessibility to nearby population centers (recreation land is an exception).

It was never truer that those who can afford the down payment on a home but prefer to rent are generally throwing their money down a rathole. Given the equity one builds as a house appreciates in value and the tax writeoff on the mortgage interest, it makes sense to stretch your finances a little to own your own home.

And if you have a little left over to invest, it also makes sense to put some of the income into, perhaps, a second home that can be rented, an apartment building, or commercial and industrial property.

The tax write-offs, for example, on apartment houses can be found in their depreciation, taxes, mortgage interest, management expenses, maintenance, and a host of other areas. Check with your Internal Revenue Service Office or your accountant on these tax advantages which you can turn into inflation hedges.

But beware of the financial dangers inherent in an apartment house investment. It looks pretty on paper to forecast that inflation will keep the value of the apartment house up, rents will pay off the loan, and the investor is left with a windfall deal. This is fine if the building stays fully rented. But you must also assess whether there is a continuing demand in the neighborhood in which you have invested. Is the city allowing the area to decay? Has industry moved in to the detriment of land values? Or, as in New York City, can rent controls freeze you into a situation where your costs and taxes are going up in the face of locked-in rents which you can't raise?

The biggest current demand appears to be for smaller rental housing—duplexes, triplexes, five- and ten-unit structures—which don't require a great deal of management and overhead. This is because the name of the game is to avoid situations where tenants are moving in and out every few months and turning the property into a "hotel." That usually leads to higher upkeep costs in the form of continuous painting and other chores to satisfy the new tenants and to make the units competitive.

Renovating rundown apartment buildings and houses also can be profitable, but you must have keen cost control if you are to stay ahead of the game. Moreover, you must make sure the building is structurally sound and, again, in a desirable location.

Picking up repossessed properties also can be a profitable venture. Keep your credit in top shape and make good contacts with banks and savings and loan associations, which from time to time have repossessions able to be picked up and refurbished at a tidy profit. These "repos" range from single-family homes to apartment houses.

Don't forget the problems of tenant militancy, which are being felt throughout the country. Tenants are fighting rent increases more than ever before against the backdrop of soaring consumer prices, and it may be next to impossible to convince your renters that you are raising rents simply to cover rising costs and taxes. In fact, this situation plus the rising costs of managing rental units has led many property owners to consider converting their units to condominiums—in effect, spinning them off at a healthy profit. But even this isn't so easy anymore. To preserve rental housing, New York City, for example, has a law prohibiting converting apartment housing into condominiums unless 35% of the tenants in the building approve. Other large urban areas are expected to consider similar measures.

Commercial property has appreciated almost as fast in recent years, at about a 20% to 30% clip in good, growing areas. Again, watch the neighborhood. Be careful, for example, that your property isn't in a section of the downtown area that is moving to more desirable locations; e.g., stores to surburban shopping centers. The value of your holding will drop proportionately. In other words, don't get yourself into a situation where the worth of your factory or office building depends on people moving *back* to make it valuable. Find a location that is growing, not one where revitalization efforts may or may *not* restore the land to its old value.

In commercial property it is very important to look at the lease arrangements. This is much more important than in a residential investment where the leases are much shorter or nonexistent. Long-term commercial leases can freeze you into a financial mess in the face of rising taxes and insurance rates. And it's the rent you are getting for that commercial property that makes it most valuable.

If you have gambler instincts, you might want to take a chance on an empty piece of commercial property—grabbing it at a low price in the expectation that the area will experience an increase in popularity, thus leading to a neighborhood boomlet.

Land speculation is a completely different ball game. If you remember nothing else about real estate, burn into your brain that one never purchases land sight unseen. Whether it's in South Dakota or South America, visit that gorgeous parcel of dream land outlined so carefully in your favorite magazine. Check public reports on the land; talk to the county recorder and other local officials and residents. Find out about the improvements such as paved roads and utilities.

Land speculation can be more of a science than shooting craps in Las Vegas. Study population movements, highway and freeway construction plans, and patterns of urban development.

Not all valuable land is located in or near a city. It may be near a growing recreation area, for example. Be sure to check, however, that the amenities of life also are present—like decent roads—if you want to see some appreciation.

A related investment is the renewed interest in country and farm land. Rural property, especially parcels within a few hours' drive of an urban center, are being looked upon more and more by city people who want to get away from the tensions of the metropolis.

Also, look to invest in the fastest-growing geographical areas of the United States. Again, anticipation of growth is the key. The key areas on the Eastern seaboard are from Delaware south to Florida. Other fast-growth areas include the Midwest and upper Midwestern states from Ohio to Wisconsin and Minnesota; and the Southwest, including Texas, Oklahoma, Wyoming. Nevada, Utah, Colorado, and Arizona.

Remember that in investing in land, if you are near or at retirement age, you probably should look to rental property or property that has income potential instead. With land you have to wait for appreciation and in the meantime there is no income.

Real estate experts say that to be profitable land should appreciate at least 10% a year. Recreational land (where you can put your second home) and suburban land (in the path of urban growth) are prime investment targets.

If you are seeking a second house for vacation or retirement, do some research on your own before you invest dollars it took you a lifetime to put together. Then when you've found that ideal country spot, check around to see if any government land is for sale. Or a national park may set aside homesites for lease which could mean big savings for you. Investigate tax lien sales that might save you a bushel of cash. And be sure to find out the potential of renting that second home if you only plan to spend a few months a year there. The rent alone could pay for the mortgage—or a good part of it—until you're ready to retire to that home or sell it. This is a big business with condominium renting in vacation and recreational areas such as Sun Valley, Idaho, and Aspen, Colorado, where management companies compete to sell condominiums as investments which you can occupy a few months a year and then rent out for the balance of the year. Chances are, if you don't want to spend the time handling the year-round rental details, these real estate companies will package the condominium deal so that, for a fee, they will see to it that your condominium is rented and producing income when you're not there.

But it's the residential home that is the closest to the heart of the average American. And with mortgage money so tight (at the time of the writing of this book) fewer homes were being built and families moving into a new home tended to hang on to their first home in many instances as an inflation hedge.

There are lots of fine points to look out for in purchasing a home, points out Don McNary, vice-president of Robbins Real Estate, a large Eastern firm located in Virginia in the shadow of the Washington, D.C., metropolitan area. One of the most important, he calls "sewerability"—that is, one must make sure when moving into a newer area that it has adequate sewers. "Ecologists have slowed down the building of new sewage treatment plants so that a developer may have a difficult time getting sewer taps," says McNary. "One would be a fool to buy anything [in a home] without adequate sewers."

Another form of real estate investment is the real estate investment trust, otherwise known as the REIT. Some $6 billion has been invested in REITs in the past decade.

A REIT is akin to a mutual fund operation. The investor buys shares of a trust, pooling his money with other investors. The operation of the REIT is by experienced real estate people who then proceed to buy apartment houses, shopping centers, commercial and industrial land, or mortgages. Thus, a small investor can become a shareholder in large real estate properties. And you have the tax deduction advantages of individual real estate ownership, which covers mortgage interest, depreciation, and property taxes.

A major pitfall: poor REIT management. Check out who's running the REIT before you leap. Study the REIT prospectus.

Additionally, high interest rates have hurt the REIT market. And market experts say the trend will continue unless interest rates drop and cash is pumped back into the construction business. As we've mentioned, the main source of money for construction, the savings and loan industry, is hurting as money is being withdrawn in favor of higher-interest-paying short-term money market instruments.

In a nutshell . . .

Rapid appreciation in real estate—homes, apartments, commercial property—can keep you ahead of the inflation level.

If you're not intimately familiar with the property or the area, study it or work through a reputable real estate firm before laying out any investment dollars.

Study population movements, trends (such as use of rural land), and an area's stability (such as an aircraft industry layoff impacting a city's economy). Make sure the area you select isn't overly dependent on one industry.

Don't load yourself up with debt just to play the real estate investment game. The American Bankers Association says the old rule of purchasing a house worth 2½ times a borrower's income may be too expensive because of rising taxes, interest, maintenance and fuel costs. The

ABA suggests 1½ times income as the new limit. The trouble with this formula, however, is that so many desirable homes now cost several times an individual's annual wage.

Don't be overconcerned with liquidity. If you've done your homework on location, you should be able to spin off the property in a maximum of 60 to 90 days.

Be careful when you land speculate. Above all else, buy nothing sight unseen.

In a residential investment, check the management costs of the property. In a commercial dwelling study the lease arrangements.

Finally, like the other investments in this book, diversify your dollars. Don't tie up all of your cash in real estate. For although the liquidity is fairly good, you may want to take advantage of short-term swings in financial markets, such as in government securities. As you will see, part of the key to investment success is to stay flexible and diversified.

Chapter IV

YOUR FRIENDLY SWISS BANKER
—Playing the Currency Game

"If you knew how many people in this city have foreign bank accounts, you'd fall off your chair."

James E. Sinclair speaks with the knowledge gathered as a partner and international trading expert at the small Wall Street firm of Vilas & Hickey, a company the public doesn't hear about because it deals with professionals—other brokers, banks, and a handful of sophisticated speculators.

"I see double-digit inflation as the trend of the world," says Sinclair. "And I think the target trend is a 15% inflation rate. It's now (April, 1974) approximately 11.5% on average ... I think the trend in England will be the trend in the United States: total capitulation to inflation ..."

Sinclair recommends inflation hedges in the form of

harder currencies than the U.S. dollar—and gold bullion, gold coins, and gold mining stocks.

So let's shift gears and move away from the more traditional investments we have been discussing. After all, they are only considered moderate inflation hedges. If, in fact, the dollar is eroding against continuing high inflation—as has been the case for the past two years—then we must be creative in our investment plans. Since hyperinflation accompanied by an economic slowdown can demolish our savings and traditional investments, perhaps the investment patterns of the 1970's and beyond have made the securities markets, real estate, and the like obsolete.

If you believe doomsday is still a long way off but see a need for new thinking on inflation hedging, this then is for you.

Set aside a few thousand investment dollars on a short-term experimental basis—as much as you can afford to *lose.* Until other market investments can neutralize or forge ahead of double-digit inflation, it's worth your time and effort to look into the following chapters of this book which are devoted to more exotic ideas which, given current world economic conditions, may soon prove to be as *de rigueur*—the thing to do—among individual investors as buying stock once was.

And if you have qualms about pulling your hard-earned cash out of your local bank or savings and loan or out of the stock market and diverting it into foreign currencies or gold-related investments, then listen to a staunch American, James E. Sinclair:

"I say the most patriotic thing I can do for my country is to remain solvent."

The first step toward remaining solvent, believes Sinclair and a growing number of other Americans, is through investment in foreign currencies.

"The biggest game in the world today isn't trading in shares," says Sinclair. "It's trading in currencies. That's where the big money will continue to be made in the next one to three years."

Today Sinclair and most other pro-foreign currency advocates are pushing the Swiss franc, which has appreciated remarkably in the past few years against two U.S. dollar devaluations to the tune of some 40%!

In 1974 alone, the Swiss franc, selling as low as $.2931 against the U.S. dollar in January, shot up to $.3586 in mid-May, a 22.3% jump and a 223% gain for an investor who bought it on 10% margin.

One major tax advantage for Americans to consider is that your foreign currency gain isn't considered taxable under capital gains tax laws until it's converted back into dollars again. That's because under the law the trade isn't completed until the dollar becomes, in effect, a dollar again and the cycle is completed.

You can purchase the Swiss franc and other foreign currency at major banks or at a currency exchange such as Deak & Co. Inc., which owns Perera Co. Inc. of New York, the big foreign exchange house. Deak also holds the majority interests in the Foreign Commerce Bank (FCB) of Zurich and Bankhaus Deak & Co. Ltd. of Vienna, Austria.

Other popular "strong" currencies against the dollar are the West German mark, the Dutch guilder, and the Austrian schilling.

Most investors in foreign currency keep the cash in a foreign bank, usually of the Swiss (and sometimes of the Austrian) variety. If one accepts the basic premise that inflation leads to chaotic financial conditions (which is why you're into the Swiss franc in the first place), then one accepts the possibility that the U.S. could enact exchange controls somewhere down the line as have other countries during periods of economic dislocation.

Of course, if Washington does come down with exchange controls we might look to the Italian experience—a country that in 1974 experienced a disintegrating economy wracked by inflation and a bankrupting $1 billion a month balance-of-payments deficit.

Italy has exchange controls. You can't carry lira out of the country except in small amounts for travel purposes. Yet on almost any given day, Italians carrying suitcases stuffed with lira might be discerned trotting across the border to Lugano, Switzerland, to queue up at one of Lugano's 39 banks. The money is usually accepted without question. (Why don't the Italian border guards stop their compatriots? There is a theory that loyalty to one's fellow townspeople is stronger than to the Italian government and its monetary problems.)

There are more subtle ploys, of course, for getting money into Switzerland. You can use a middleman from a country that doesn't have exchange controls. This individual, for a fee (in Europe it runs 10% or more), will open an account for you. Stories abound in Europe of a growing corps of professionals who have taken on this function. They range from ex-CIA agents to a German mutual fund manager.

Businessmen have used "double invoices" (where the party receiving the invoices forwards one to a Swiss bank) and dummy corporations in Liechtenstein or the Caribbean to hide money tracks into Switzerland.

The moral to this is that exchange controls have dubious value.

Other advantages of maintaining a Swiss account accrue from the famous Swiss tradition of banking secrecy. Therefore, you really don't need a numbered account in Switzerland—and, furthermore, not all Swiss banks allow Americans to open a numbered account and, if they do, it has to be done in person.

A fabled numbered account really doesn't amount to very much. It just means that a handful, maybe two or three, of a Swiss bank's top officers have access to the identity of the account, which makes a leak less likely. But even with a standard Swiss bank account, you have more privacy than you generally enjoy in the United States. The Swiss simply believe that a person's bank account is no one else's business. This means that the Swiss government doesn't have access to a bank's computer records. And, under Swiss law, a bank employe can face a tough fine and jail sentence if the individual reveals information about an account to anyone not in the employ of the bank.

To the extent that another government can prove to Swiss legal authorities that an individual was using the Swiss banking system to hide money obtained through robbery, kidnapping, drug trade, and the like, the Swiss will cooperate with foreign governments.

But the Swiss must also view the crime as a felony under their own laws. Thus, a foreign government probably wouldn't get much, if any, cooperation on tax or foreign exchange evasion charges.

More practical reasons for opening a Swiss bank account include the fact that Swiss bank reserves are generally higher than those in the U.S.; and you can easily participate in European and other international financial markets through a highly efficient banking system. Minimum bank account requirements in Switzerland range from $1,-000 or less to several thousand dollars.

One professional foreign investor says the only major problem with a Swiss bank account (which he thinks should be part of your investment thinking) is the time difference between the U.S. and Zurich. "You can't call your Swiss banker at a reasonable hour of the day," he quips.

The Swiss, of course, are delighted to see all of this foreign cash finding its way into those cool Swiss vaults, especially during times of international unrest and high inflation. It makes the tiny nation wealthy. "We don't care where the money comes from, or how it gets here," one Swiss banker was quoted. "But we do hate to take and invest illegal money."

The banker meant the Swiss don't want cash obtained under circumstances that would brand the person as a criminal in Switzerland.

By mid-1974 (according to the Swiss Central Bank) Swiss bank coffers had swelled to over $80 billion which was scattered among the tiny nations top 72 banks. The five largest Swiss banks tripled their assets in the last decade. And no one knows how much additional foreign cash is in Swiss banking hands being invested for clients in everything from gold to stocks to commodities to currency futures.

Nicholas L. Deak, the international banking authority who heads Deak & Co., asserts that even though Switzerland experienced a 10% inflation in 1973, it is still the best place to keep one's money. Deak feels there is almost no possibility that the Swiss franc will be devalued in the near future. But, most Swiss banking experts don't see much advantage in opening a Swiss bank account in dollars unless it is for practical purposes involving foreign travel.

Otto E. Roethenmund, Deak executive vice-president as well as a Swiss banker, says the only perceivable reason some Americans are opening U.S. dollar-denominated accounts in Swiss banks is that they aren't interested in investing in foreign currency but simply want some money out of the country in case Washington, facing a monetary crisis, clamps down with exchange controls.

Roethenmund recalls that a number of years ago, President Lyndon B. Johnson told Americans that the nation was in for tough economic times. Johnson raised the possibility of travel and exchange restrictions. "For weeks we [the Swiss banks] couldn't handle the business," Roethenmund recalls, as Americans swamped the Swiss with orders for foreign accounts.

Commenting on the upswing in business of Americans wanting Swiss bank accounts, Thomas F. Kelly, who manages the Los Angeles office of Deak & Co., says: "I get the feeling that people don't just want to make money, they want to save what they've earned all their lives. They are interested in maintaining the buying power of what they have on hand."

Frank H. Blankenheim, Kelly's assistant manager, adds that opening a Swiss account is almost becoming commonplace, although there are some bizarre moments.

Recently, remembered Blankenheim, a young man marched into Deak's downtown Los Angeles office, threw a large suitcase on the counter, and asked for an account in the Foreign Commerce Bank of Zurich.

He then proceeded to reveal $200,000 in cash in the suitcase in $10 and $20 bills. The account was quickly opened without any hitches, recalls Blankenheim.* The only problem, he adds, was that his fingers "got cramped" from all that counting! To be sure, this is an extreme example. The procedures are usually much more routine.

Of course, some investors, as in anything else, don't exert good common sense in this sort of investing. No one is saying that *all* of your savings should be washed into Swiss francs. As we mentioned before, the prudent investor diversifies his holdings so that he can hedge against unforeseen circumstances. This includes having cash on hand for day-to-day bills.

Once, remembers Kelly, a lady came into the Deak office with 20 German marks she wanted to convert into dollars, declaring, "I have to change this into U.S. dollars because I want to go to the grocery store." The woman

---

*Actually, Deak itself doesn't directly open the Swiss bank account for you because it isn't licensed to do so. But by putting you in touch with a Swiss bank and by providing you with the proper forms, it is, in effect, doing the same thing.

had converted *all* of her savings into marks. An extreme example, of course, but it makes the point that short of picking up and moving to Switzerland, you still must have some change in your pocket to exist in America, no matter how high the rate of inflation.

Opening the account is quite easy. In fact. except for the distance between you and the Swiss bank. the routine differs little from asking for an account at First National City Bank or Bank of America.

You can get the names and addresses of the major Swiss banks from either the Swiss embassy in Washington, a Swiss consulate official, or from any one of a number of large U.S. banks. Then send a letter directly to the Swiss bank of your choice telling the kind of account you want.

Or you can have an agency like Deak's help you do it. If you open an account, for example, at Deak's Foreign Commerce Bank, you can fill out the application at any Deak office. Deak charges anywhere from $2.50 to $12.50 for processing the account, depending on the amount of your deposit, plus $5.50 for cabling the money. Here is an example of an application for opening a foreign bank account:

BANKHAUS DEAK & CO. LTD.

Application for Account Opening

(*Please type or print*)

TO: Date. . . . .
Bankhaus Deak & Co. Ltd.
Postfach 306
A-1011 Vienna, Austria

[63]

Gentlemen:

I wish to open the following account(s):

___ Checking Account in . . . .(Currency)

___ Savings Passbook Account . . . .(Currency)

___ Twin Account in . . . .(Currency)

___ I wish to purchase an International Certificate of Deposit in the amount of . . . . for a period of ____3 months ____6 months ____12 months

I enclose a check for . . . . payable to your bank.

The account is to be maintained

___ under a number   ___ in my own name

___ in the name of . . . . : . . . .

Side 2 of the application for opening a foreign bank account:

FROM: . . . .

                (Legal Name in full)

. . . .

                (Street address)

. . . .

                (City, State, Zip)

. . . .

                (Telephone area code and number)

Personal Data:

Citizenship . . . .

Passport No. . . . .

Bank advices, statements, correspondence, etc., should be

___ mailed to me   ___ held at the bank

Language to be used is: ___ English   ___ German

The beneficiaries of this account, in the event of the account holder's death are: . . . .

. . . .

. . . .

. . . .

Please address your mail as follows:
___ As mentioned above

___ . . . .
. . . .
. . . .

Sincerely yours,

_____

(Signature)

Here is a copy of a signature card you would receive from a Swiss or Austrian bank:

Bankhaus Deak & Co. Ltd.

Kontoinhaber
Account Holder(s) . . . . No. . . . . . .
     (Name(n) in Blockschrift/Name(s) in
     Block Letters)
Verfügungsberechtigte Person(en) über mein/unser Konto:
Person(s) authorized to sign validly on my/our behalf:

Name and Vorname	Unterschriften/	einzeln oder
Name and Surname	Signatures	koll. zu zweien
		sign singly
		or jointly

_____

_____

_____

_____

Ich (wir) bestätige(n) eine Kopie der Allgemeinen Geschäftsbedingungen erhalten zu haben und anerkenne(n) diese Bedingungen.
I (we) confirm having received a copy of the Gen-

[65]

eral Banking Conditions and agree with same.
Datum:
Date: ....
       Unterschrift(en) des/der Kontoinhaber(s)
       Signature(s) of Account Holder(s)

The so-called big three of the Swiss banking industry include Union Bank, Swiss Bank Corporation, and Swiss Credit Bank. They have branch banking in Switzerland and outlets in New York and other U.S. cities.*

When writing to one of these or any other publicly operated Swiss bank, have your signature notarized by an office of the bank in the U.S., by a notary in the Swiss embassy or consulate, or by a U.S. bank that has an affiliation with the Swiss bank to which you are applying.

Here are the addresses of the four Swiss banks mentioned here (out of over 400 Swiss banks):

> Foreign Commerce Bank
> Bellariastrasse 82
> 8038 Zurich, Switzerland
>
> Union Bank of Switzerland
> Bahnhofstrasse 45
> 8021 Zurich, Switzerland
>
> Swiss Bank Corporation
> Aeschenvorstadt 1
> 4002 Basel, Switzerland

*You probably wouldn't qualify for the private or family banks in Switzerland, which are very selective about their customers and which usually want only large accounts. In many respects. these banks operate like U.S. money managers, investing your money through a diversified portfolio.

Swiss Credit Bank
Paradeplatz
8022 Zurich, Switzerland

If you don't wish to go through an intermediary such as Deak, simply send a letter to one of these banks (with your signature notarized) and enclose a bank money order. Also be sure to tell the bank what kind of currency you want your money kept in.

To repeat, given the strength of the Swiss franc against the dollar, you're much better off keeping your savings in francs if you decide to open a foreign bank account. The interest rate will be lower in francs, but the appreciation has made up for this many times over in recent years (for example, the Foreign Commerce Bank allows 4% annual interest on a Swiss franc account against a 6% annual rate for a U.S. dollar account).*

You'll soon receive correspondence from the Swiss bank you selected. including a receipt of deposit. In future correspondence all you need do is use your account number to transact business. And, as is the case with American banks, the account can be just in your name or in more than one name. Withdrawing the funds, either by letter or cable, is just as simple.

You won't have to worry about the language barrier, either. The Swiss banking industry has done international business since time immemorial, and most of the banks—certainly the large ones—correspond in English.

Vilas & Hickey's Sinclair has some other theories about

* As of Oct. 31, 1974, Swiss banking authorities imposed a 12% levy—or "negative" interest rate—on new money deposited in that country to slow down the flow of speculative funds.

[67]

corresponding with the Swiss, however. First, he says, "There must be a special school for Swiss bankers where they teach them to scribble. You can never read their names." Then there's the theory that letters to depositors are typewritten, but the signature is scribbled without being typewritten underneath to discourage foreigners from directly corresponding with Swiss bankers. The Swiss, so it would appear, want to keep their system insulated from the rest of the world.

Secondly, quips Sinclair, "The Swiss are extremely courteous but their English, a translation of German, comes out like an order from a panzer tank commander—it's not what we would call courteous but certainly very businesslike."

As is the case with American banks, you can get a number of different accounts and services from a Swiss bank. Using Deak's Foreign Commerce Bank as an example, here's what's available:

Current Account (checking account). If you are staying primarily in the U.S., this probably isn't for you. The minimum deposit is $1,500 or the equivalent in foreign currencies. A current account draws *no* interest. An individual's funds may be withdrawn at any time without notice.

Deposit Account (savings account). This account is probably best suited to your needs if you want to open an account in Swiss francs. The minimum deposit is $4,000 or the equivalent in foreign currencies (this may vary widely). The interest on a Swiss franc or German mark account is 4% per annum and 7% on U.S. dollars. You can withdraw up to $1,500 per month without any prior notice; from $1,501 to $3,000 with 30 days' notice; and above $3,000 with 60 days' notice.

Certificates of Deposit. These may be sold in U.S. dollars or foreign currencies. The minimum certificate of deposit at FCB is $500 or foreign equivalent, with the following interest rates as of March 1, 1974:

	U.S. Dollar	Dutch Guilder	German Mark	British Pound
Three months	7%	7%	6½%	15%
Six months	7¼%	7½%	7%	14%
Nine months	7½%	8%	7½%	13%

At the time of this writing there was no certificate of deposit available in Swiss francs with a Swiss bank but Swiss franc certificates could be purchased through Austrian banks.

In addition, you may wish to keep your securities in a Swiss bank. If you do, the minimum charge is $2.50 at the FCB with an annual charge for safekeeping and administration of 0.125% of the market value of the securities for clients residing outside of Switzerland.

Other services include portfolio management, commodity trading ($1,000 minimum), metal trading (on the New York, London and Zurich markets), and mutual funds (involving most American and international investment funds). In the latter case, a $1,000 minimum investment is required. Banking charges include a $10 initial fee plus 0.375% of the invested amount plus nominal liquidation charges.

Swiss banks will also store certain commodities for you such as silver bars or gold coins.

A Swiss federal withholding tax of 30% is deducted from the interest paid on savings accounts. But since Switzerland and the United States have a double-taxation treaty, you can obtain a form from your Swiss bank, file it with the Swiss government, and get a refund of ⅚, or 25% of your tax.

A few years ago the Swiss became concerned about the inflationary impact of the wave of currency flowing into Swiss banks from weaker currency nations and imposed a negative interest tax on checking and savings accounts. The tax came to 2% per quarter for the privilege of opening a Swiss account. But the tax was generally removed in the fall of 1973. At publication, an individual could deposit up to 50,000 Swiss francs—$16,000 to $17,000— and draw about 4% annual interest. Anything over the 50,000 franc level in the same account simply wouldn't draw interest. This policy is a fluctuating one, however, and you should check with the bank with which you wish to do business.

Of course, you could open several accounts under 50,-000 francs at different Swiss banks to take advantage of the positive interest rate. But remember, even without that 4% you are still way ahead of the game because, as we said, the Swiss franc has shown remarkable appreciation against the dollar.

If you wish to retain and maintain the privacy of a Swiss account you might want to pass up the tax rebate you get through the double-taxation agreement between the U.S. and Switzerland. It's conceivable that certain information about your Swiss account could be recorded by Washington, which is notified in the process of the Swiss refunding the ⅚ of the 30% Swiss tax on your bank account interest. When compared to the appreciation of the franc, the amount isn't significant anyway.

FCB's Roethenmund says it's not very important to diversify your currency portfolio. "Pick a popular currency such as the Swiss franc, German mark, or maybe the Dutch guilder," says Roethenmund, "but stick to one, because if the Swiss franc moves up, so does the mark and the guilder."

Roethenmund, who has an extensive background in the field of international exchange, says investors also ought to take a look at the way the professionals play the international currency field by rolling over 30-, 60-, and 90-day Eurocurrency certificates of deposit denominated in "hard" currencies such as the Swiss franc. (The only basic difference between these CDs and U.S. bank CDs is the currency denomination.) An individual can instruct the bank whether to roll over Eurocurrency contracts extending up to 12 months or more (the professionals like to stay on the short end and certainly no more than 12 months), and if you wish your bank will automatically purchase new certificates when the old ones reach maturity. Your Swiss bank can also arrange to buy and deposit Eurocurrency accounts outside of Switzerland.

For example, many currency pros prefer to see their certificates of deposit in Austrian banks such as Creditanstalt, Laenderbank, and Bankhaus Deak. Although the Swiss banking system is one of the soundest in the world, there are some advantages to using the nearby Austrian banking system.

First of all, Austrian interest rates on certificates of deposit were generally higher at this writing than Swiss certificates.

Second, the Austrians don't deduct any taxes from the interest on certificates in contrast to the 30% Swiss tax.

Austrian bank certificates of deposit offer you a way to participate in foreign exchange action because they can be denominated in any currency. "An investor who purchased an Austrian certificate in Swiss francs in 1971 would have made 40% on his money by May, 1974," said Sinclair, "and that's just from rate changes. It doesn't include the interest payments."

The Austrian certificates of deposit run from $500 to $5 million. By buying them directly from an Austrian bank, investors eliminate brokerage fees.

One must remember, however, currency speculation can also be a very dangerous game. Like any other commodity, rates may go up quickly but they can plummet just as rapidly. And when you play with margin (where you only put up the down payment) you just might find yourself owing a lot more than you bargained for.

For the novice, it's best to start with your Swiss or Austrian savings account denominated in Swiss francs or one of the other strong currencies mentioned here. If that whets your appetite, the certificate route is a fairly solid investment. The high rollers play with currency futures, but that's no place for beginners.

Be aware that the U.S. government requires American banks to report overseas transfers in excess of $5,000. Check with your banker or lawyer if you have any questions.

Also check with your accountant or lawyer about IRS rules on listing foreign bank accounts on your tax return.

You don't have to send your money abroad to get into exchange rate futures action. Chicago's International Monetary Market trades futures contracts in currencies as if they were commodities such as pork bellies or soybeans. Currency expert Sinclair believes, however, the Chicago market is too limited. A currency contract holder, says Sinclair, can't always get out when he wants.

"The way the big money does it," says Sinclair, "is to buy forward currency contracts on an interbank basis." The first requirement is an account with a foreign-based international bank. (U.S.-based banks, apparently under instructions from the Federal Reserve Board, don't get involved in individual forward currency deals, but do accept orders from American companies that want to hedge commercial transactions.)

Sinclair explains that the interbank market works like a futures market. "Bank A on your behalf contracts with Bank B for delivery of Swiss francs in one month, three months, six months or a year. You can get out anytime by entering a short contract with Bank C to deliver the same number of francs on a date closely corresponding to the delivery date of the first contract."

Sound complicated? You're right! Unless you have some of Sinclair's expertise.

In a nutshell . . .

Opening a Swiss or Austrian bank account is about as simple as opening one with an American bank. Denominate your account in Swiss francs, which is expected to remain a strong currency at least for the next few years. Thus, you'll be realizing the appreciation of the franc plus about 4% interest. It's the easiest way for the foreign currency novice to get his or her feet wet.

Check with representatives of the big three Swiss banks in the U.S. or the Swiss embassy on any questions you might have. Another source is Otto E. Roethenmund, the Deak and Foreign Commerce Bank representative and an expert on how to reap benefits from investing in foreign currency and opening foreign bank accounts. He can be reached in New York at 212-425-6789; or in Zurich at telephone number 45 66 88.

If you want to play the currency markets more actively, instruct your bank to "roll over" your cash in Eurocurrency certificates of deposit. Or, a riskier venture, would be to play the currency futures game.

In all cases remember, as fast as many currencies appreciate, they can "correct" themselves and plummet. You stand to lose as well as gain. Invest only as much as you can afford to miss from your day-to-day living. Set aside cash that is lying dormant in a savings account. Start with maybe 10% or 20%.

Look at it this way: Money alone won't make you happy—unless it's in Switzerland!

Chapter V

THE GOLD (AND SILVER) RUSH . . . 1970's STYLE
—*Investing in Gold and Silver*

The new gold cult is a direct outgrowth of our current unstable economic conditions. It tells us that uncounted individuals have lost faith in paper currencies and the traditional forms of investments in which we put our money. Members of the Gold Club consistently warn that investing in gold is not the doomsday approach to hedging one's investments—it is the *only* approach to economic survival. Among these prophets are Franz Pick, the international gold observer, Harry Schultz, one of the world's most widely quoted gold watchers, and James Dines, whose newsletter has been espousing gold and gold-related investments for years. All of these well-educated gentlemen look for the U.S. economy to completely capitulate to inflation. And gold, they say, represents *the* fundamental defense to the chaos they say will surely follow this surrender.

Two devaluations of the dollar and the ensuing serious worldwide inflation have indeed convinced swarms of investors that if the banks don't open tomorrow, gold may be the only recourse. They have been influenced by the goldbugs' argument that the yellow metal is the only reliable money and the only way to measure a nation's true wealth.

The scenario the goldbugs foresee is a grim one. It involves uncontrollable inflation leading to worthless paper currencies. The dollar itself ultimately becomes worthless. Gold, ranging near $200 an ounce in 1974, shoots up to $500, $1,000 an ounce, and even higher. There is a total breakdown of the economy. Businesses and banks collapse by the thousands. The stock market is crushed. A severe depression grips the world. Violence in the streets. Revolutions. Build a retreat and try to weather the storm in the knowledge your investments are safe in gold buried in the ground or cooling off in a Swiss vault, cry the gloom and doomers.

I take a more moderate view.

The goldbugs have been predicting the end for decades now. Granted, the scope of the current worldwide inflation is of serious dimensions. It has people worried, which is why the books and seminars of these prophets of doom are selling out.

"Although gold may not be in the International Monetary Fund's plans for the future, it's in people's minds psychologically," says Deak's Tom Kelly.

Certainly, the policies of Washington, which include

pumping more money into the economy in attempts to maintain prosperity, have fueled inflation. But the thesis of the goldbugs that currencies—if they are to have any value—must be directly linked to gold isn't necessarily the answer.

Many economists feel that a country's natural resources, its industry, and the productivity of its labor force are more important than what they consider to be the medieval value of gold. It is the strength of a nation and the confidence of its people in its government which controls the viability of a currency, says this school of economic thought.

Currency has value because people have faith in it *and* the country issuing the money. It has been so for centuries. We don't evaluate currencies because they are backed 10% or 40% by gold. Government policies establish the value of paper money. Should governments capitulate to inflation, I doubt we'll be using chips of gold at the corner supermarket. Adjustments of currencies by governments and international bodies such as the International Monetary Fund will still be the rule. Even at the height of the terrible inflation levels of Germany's Weimar Republic, a true barter society was not achieved.

"The goldbugs' story is somewhat fascinating but it's a little bit of economic science fiction," says Leif Olsen, First National City Bank economist. "In economics, fear always sells better than optimism. If somebody yells 'fire' in a theater, some people run for the exit, whether there is a fire or not. I don't think there's any grounds for that kind of fear. I see no economic collapse in the U.S. and no collapse of the international monetary system."

Nevertheless, for those investors who are looking to hedge against sustained double-digit inflation, gold bullion gold mining shares, and gold (and silver) coins (which we will discuss in the next chapter) have provided a good return during the past year. I mention gold bullion for the American readers of this book because the Congress approved and President Ford signed into law legislation allowing Americans to own gold for the first time in 40 years.

But be wary of the doomsday approach that says gold is the *only* answer to inflation protection and which calls for diverting most of your investment dollars into the yellow metal. To do so is asking for a lot of trouble. Gold, like any other commodity, is subject to price corrections that can wipe the average investor out in a short time.

André Sharon of the Wall Street firm of Drexel Burnham & Co., who doesn't consider himself a goldbug, suggests that a fairly conservative 15% of an investor's cash should be in gold mining issues (which we will discuss later in this chapter).

But Sharon also emphasizes that the individual investor is taking a big risk in gold issues. The price of gold and gold stocks is greatly influenced by emotional issues, thus making it difficult to rationally predict their behavior, says Sharon. Recently (mid-1974) he says he has noticed some of the "smart" or professional money pulling out of gold issues.

In one year alone, 1969, Sharon observes that Standard & Poor's gold issue index plunged almost 60% and took years to bounce back.

As you probably already know, the official price of

gold—the price which governs transactions between governments or central banks—is $42.22 an ounce. The private market price, however, has been soaring, breaking the $180 an ounce level in February of 1974, receding to the $150's by mid-1974 and then bouncing up again to the $180's toward the end of the year. Washington, of course, wants to play down the role of gold in any new monetary order. And the IMF in June of 1974 took a big step in that direction by enacting several international monetary reforms. Ultimately, the IMF would like Special Drawing Rights—called "paper gold"—to replace the metal. But there are still several world leaders who believe that gold has a place in a new monetary order. The French, for example, have long worshipped the metal.

To be sure, gold has a history of being accepted as the international monetary backing for currency. Until the Depression of the 1930's, Americans were allowed to hoard as much gold as they wanted. Gold coins worth $1 and up were legal tender. But President Franklin D. Roosevelt's pump priming policies ended all that; the economy needed paper currency, and by 1934, through the Gold Reserve Act, ownership of gold bullion, except for industrial purposes, was declared illegal.

Then, on August 14, 1974, President Ford lifted this gold ban. The legislation allowed Americans to own gold bullion by the end of the year. Language in the bill gave Mr. Ford the option of permitting private gold ownership before December 31, 1974, if he decided that negotiations with other nations on monetary reform had reached the point "where elimination of regulations on private ownership of gold will not adversely affect the United States' international monetary position."

On the other hand, Treasury Secretary William E. Simon said the Administration could seek a delay of that December 31 deadline if it felt that removing the gold curb might prove damaging to monetary reform and international monetary markets.

Most goldwatchers expect that when the gold ownership date becomes a reality, a spurt in gold demand will push the price of the metal up about 10% or a little more before a correction sets in.

For thousands of years, people have traditionally turned to gold during times of political upheaval and financial uncertainty. The goldbugs therefore judge a nation's currency by the amount of gold held in their vaults.

Gold holdings of the world's leading industrial nations are shown in the chart which appears on page 81.

The gold holdings of these nations are, in effect, frozen until the International Monetary Fund can decide what role, if any, the metal should play in the world's monetary system.

Thus, the U.S. has about $11.6 billion worth of gold. To protect this supply from the $80 billion dollar "overhang" abroad (called Eurodollars), our government closed the gold window on August 15, 1971—we simply stopped trading in gold. Washington didn't have enough gold to pay out to foreigners who might want to cash in their dollars. It was the Nixon Administration's way of meeting its growing balance of payments and trade deficits. Two dollar devaluations were to follow.

The goldbugs maintain that the situation has consider-

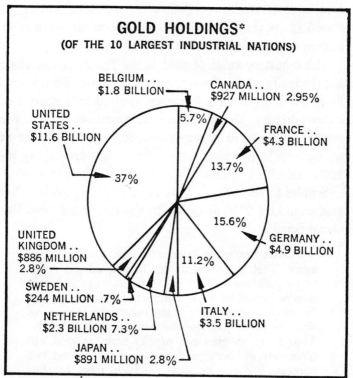

GOLD HOLDINGS*
(OF THE 10 LARGEST INDUSTRIAL NATIONS)

BELGIUM ..
$1.8 BILLION
5.7%

CANADA ..
$927 MILLION 2.95%

UNITED
STATES ..
$11.6 BILLION
37%

FRANCE ..
$4.3 BILLION
13.7%

15.6%

GERMANY ..
$4.9 BILLION

UNITED
KINGDOM ..
$886 MILLION
2.8%

11.2%

SWEDEN ..
$244 MILLION .7%

NETHERLANDS ..
$2.3 BILLION 7.3%

ITALY ..
$3.5 BILLION

JAPAN ..
$891 MILLION 2.8%

* Held by central banks and governments of non-Communist nations;
valued at $42.22 per fine ounce.

ably worsened. Aside from the fact that they see less than 4% of total U.S. currency in circulation in the world backed by gold (as opposed to, say, Switzerland with a 70% ratio), they see the Arab grip on oil supplies exacerbating the monetary situation. The Arabs, claim the goldbugs, may also come to distrust paper currency to the point where they will demand gold for oil, thus pushing up gold prices. Thus far, however, the Arabs have been content to reinvest their dollars and other currencies received in payment for oil into short-term money market instruments in Europe and the United States.

The monetary value of gold in the private marketplace is principally set in the markets of London, Zurich, and Paris. As demand for gold grows, spurred by a distrust of paper currency, the price rises. If confidence (a delicate flower) increases in paper currencies, gold will not be as widely sought by those who believe they are fleeing inflated, unstable currencies.

Schultz forecast in his February, 1974, newsletter that gold would hit $210 an ounce by the end of the year. Declared Schultz:

> Politics has often interfered with gold and may again. That is the risk factor in projecting a price. Some politicos will try to stop gold again, before they're buried by it. But market forces are powerful. So I conclude that if the inflation rate rises, so will the yellow metal—our main link with reality. Thus I say no man can predict how far gold will *ultimately* go, because nobody can see around two corners. We can estimate inflation rates for this year but to go two-three years ahead is guesswork and assumes no change of trend is possible. It also requires knowledge of the rate of change, i.e., whether the inflation rate accelerates or decelerates. These are unknowables. And as we live only in the present, it's really enough to know the trend is "up" without knowing whether gold is going to $160 or six times that . . . $210 gold appears likely now, based on present escalation of inflation rate. When it will come is secondary. There will be several down moves along the way. Prudent investors will trade all along this golden highway.*

The International Harry Schultz Letter, February, 1974, p. 2.

James Dines, editor of *The Dines Letter*, takes a similar goldbug approach. Sell all your common stocks and bonds, get some money into a Swiss bank in Swiss francs or gold coins, and pump the rest of your cash into gold and silver stocks. Dines predicts the price of gold will soar to between $400 and $1,000. He is convinced that the world's monetary system, which essentially cut loose of gold when the U.S. closed its gold window in 1971, must again return to gold as the basic measure of value. Otherwise, contends Dines, you have a fiat currency, where money is printed at will and where you have more and more paper chasing the same amount of goods.

Whether or not you agree with Dines, Schultz and the other goldbugs, you still may want to hedge your investment cash against inflation to the tune of 15% or more of your portfolio. Here are the avenues open to you:

> *Gold bullion* (refined gold bars or wafers)—As we have mentioned, at this writing gold ownership for Americans was scheduled to become effective on December 31, 1974.
> *Silver bullion*
> *Gold mining stocks*
> *Gold and silver coins*

We'll look at the first three options in this chapter and save the coins for the next one.

Until December 31, 1974, or until the Ford Administration gives the official go-ahead for American gold ownership, the nearest outlet to the United States for gold bullion purchases is Canada.

Should gold ownership become a reality, one could purchase the yellow metal at commercial banks, for example, and store it either at the bank or at an independent warehouse facility—unless you would like to keep a day-to-day eye on your bullion in your home wall safe.

Additionally, gold futures sales would commence at the same time.

Both the Chicago Board of Trade and the International Monetary Market of the Chicago Mercantile Exchange have announced they are ready to start trading in gold futures a few days after the law goes into effect. Similar arrangements were being made on the New York Mercantile Exchange and that city's Commodity Exchange (COMEX).

Europeans have been buying gold freely for years. Many goldwatchers suspect that Americans, too, have been buying gold illegally at Swiss and perhaps some Canadian banks and storing it in those banks. If the Swiss banks ask no questions, it would be difficult for Washington to prevent such transactions.

If you purchase bullion through a Swiss bank, it may be weighed in grams or ounces. One gram equals .03215 ounces; one kilogram equals 32.15 ounces.

Some Swiss banks require a minimum gold bullion purchase of a 400 ounce bar (12½ kilograms). If the price of gold is $150 an ounce, the price tag on a 400 ounce bar would then be $60,000.

Many Swiss banks will allow you to buy gold bullion in smaller amounts. These smaller bars or wafers may come in sizes ranging from 10 to 1,000 grams each. Swiss banks generally will only store a substantial gold purchase, so if you want to store the smaller wafers you'll have to do it in your own safety deposit box or mount an ingot on the coffee table as a conversation piece.

It isn't known to what extent American investors will divert their stock and bond holdings and savings into gold wafers and bars once gold ownership is legalized in the U.S.

But, quips Robert Stovall, a vice president of Reynolds Securities Inc., gold would certainly become the *in* subject of talk on the cocktail circuit.

"To own gold would be the new American status symbol," says Stovall, an astute observer of Wall Street trading patterns.

In computing the amount you pay for the bullion, remember that world market prices fluctuate as they do for any other commodity. Also remember that there may be a 30% or more markup between the wholesale and retail price.

Gold mining stocks have been rising to new highs along with the price of bullion and coins.

But unless you have some degree of expertise in these issues, it might be best to go to a gold fund. This way if you encounter trouble with one mining company, you haven't put all your ingots in one basket.

Trouble comes in many forms with gold mining stocks. And until that gold ore is out of the ground at a profit, it's just another piece of rock which has no impact on the shares of the mine in which you invested.

There is also the possibility of mine strikes and other labor problems, natural disasters, government interference in the marketplace, and, like any other company, poor management.

Beware of making money overnight on gold bonanzas. Stick with the blue chip mining companies. Remember that the cost of sinking shafts and digging tunnels may be hundreds of thousands of dollars. Construction may take years, not months. And as we shall discuss, the longevity of the mine is extremely important.

You may run into situations—sparked by the rocketing price of gold—where you are asked to invest in so-called "one man, one hole" operations involving the reopening of a once "thriving" old mine. Your chances of making a fortune overnight as a shareholder are practically nil. In Canada this sort of investment in securities with bargain basement prices has picked up the name "penny stock." Declares the Wall Street brokerage firm of Roberts, Scott and Co., Inc. about penny stocks:

> Investors should be careful about buying "cheapies," extremely low-priced "penny" stocks in purported gold mines, or mines which at best are marginal and probably very short-lived. As public attention is focused on gold, such "cheapies" get part of the limelight, sometimes through the encouragement of unknowledgeable securities salesmen. In our opinion, investors tempted by "cheapies" would be far better advised to put their money into the mutual funds specializing in gold . . .

Amen!

Before we begin listing individual gold mines, let us take a look at how the professionals operate and make their selections.

Three gold funds are:

International Investors Inc.
420 Lexington Avenue
New York, NY 10017
Tel: 212-532-4197

ASA Ltd. (formerly American South African), a
gold investment trust listed on the New York
Stock Exchange

Research Capital Fund
235 Montgomery Street
San Francisco, CA 94104
Tel: 415-989-7380

International Investors began operations in 1955 and
switched 90% of its investments into gold mining shares in
1969. The minimum individual investment is $1,000 with
subsequent increments in the amount of $100.

John C. Van Eck, the chairman of the fund. says that
his operation primarily invests in South African mines because, logically, about three-quarters of the world's gold
supply comes from that country. "What's important is the
grade of ore, the tonnage [production], and the life of the
mine." says Van Eck.

Then, he says, his fund managers attempt to project the
gold price, gold mining costs of the mine, and the price-
earnings ratio of the mining company.

You must make some basic assumptions, says Van Eck.

If you assume the U.S. will soon make the dollar con-
vertible into gold at, say, $250 an ounce, then you may
want a productive short-life mine—one that may be
mined out within 10 years—for maximum appreciation

with the thought that gold would plateau in price for the near term and then maybe dip.

If you calculate that gold will continue to rise in price over the next few years and then level off as the rate of inflation moderates, Van Eck recommends a medium-life mine.

Finally, if you foresee the gold price increasing at a rate of 10% a year for the rest of our lives, then you want a long-life mine.

Van Eck says there aren't very many gold funds in the U.S., simply because Americans are not as gold-conscious as Europeans. If American investors want a solid inflation hedge, he recommends investing up to 20% of your portfolio in gold mining shares.

Apparently a lot of people are taking his advice. Some 15,000 investors had poured $150 million into International Investors by the end of 1973, more than double the 1972 level. And, says Van Eck, their money appreciated 90% over in one year.

Van Eck boasts in his firm's annual report that if on February 10, 1956, you made an investment in his fund of $10,000 and reinvested income dividends and capital gains distributions, on December 31, 1973, it would have grown to $88,228 (if income dividends and capital gains distributions were not reinvested his calculated figure of growth is $44,953).

The advisory fee of the fund is about 8% for your initial $1,000 purchase and grows progressively smaller with larger investments.

R. Martin Wiskemann, portfolio manager and vice-president of Research Capital, a subsidiary of Franklin

Research, Inc., says gold is an excellent hedge "as insurance against catastrophe."

Wiskemann, born in Switzerland and a close observer of the gold scene for the past 20 years, says he likes to look for long life in a mine—25 years or more of productivity.

South African gold mines are a favorite of Wiskemann's. He says the accounting procedures there are good and the government's control of the mining industry has left it scandal-free. Moreover, he says, South African gold mines, the world's largest, are well capitalized and their earnings estimates are usually on the conservative side.

There are some observers of the South African gold mining industry who are bothered, however, by government control of the mines. If that government were to alter the earnings of the mines in any way it would, of course, directly impact gold mining shares.

Political unrest, not currently a problem, could someday be an unsettling factor given South Africa's apartheid policy.

Never before has there been so much interest in gold mining stocks, observes Wiskemann. "Brokers are getting checks in the mail for $5,000 with notes saying 'buy me the fund,'" he says. "And without even receiving a prospectus. This has never happened before."

The minimum investment for Research Capital is $100. Again, there are investment advisory fees.

South African golds have been paying 6 to 7% dividends every six months, says Wiskemann, while American and Canadian gold mines* have been averaging about 1%

---

* Gold shares took a tumble after this section was written, but have been firming up again.

on a quarterly basis. The short-lived mines have more substantial dividends than the longer-lived ones.

Examples of the increase in the dividends of South African golds in 1974: Doornfontein from 45 cents to 98 cents; Vaal Reefs, 75 cents to $1.50; East Rand Proprietary, 18 cents to $1.12.

Western Hemisphere gold mines have fared well, too. Witness the dividend jumps in 1974 of Campbell Red Lake Mines Ltd. to 53 cents against 19 cents for the first quarter of 1973; and Dome Mines Ltd. to $1.05 a share from 39 cents.

Wiskemann says the big attractions of South African golds is their size—much larger than any American or Canadian mine. "Because of certain favorable geological conditions, production costs are far less than those in the U.S.," he adds.

James Sinclair of Vilas & Hickey agrees. "South Africa's mining industry makes available more technical and financial data than any other industry in the world," he says. "At any given rise in the price of gold, you can work out the approximate life of the mine, the ores that will be mined, and their grades. In no other industry in the world can you so accurately evaluate the worth of a share."

Productive gold mines in the Western Hemisphere include the 100-year-old Homestake Mining Co. of Lead, South Dakota, the largest in the U.S., whose stock climbed to a high of 99⅜ in January of 1974, up more than 450% since 1971; and Campbell Red Lake, controlled by Dome Mines. Campbell Red Lake, like Homestake, is traded on the Big Board and is the largest and richest

Canadian gold operation. Campbell's stock is up 360% and Dome's 250% since 1971.

Here are the gold holdings of International Investors as of December 31, 1973:

LONG-LIFE GOLD MINES

Buffelsfontein
Doornfontein
East Driefontein
Hartebeestfontein
Kloof Gold Mining Co. Ltd.
President Steyn
Randfontein Estates
St. Helena Gold Mines, Ltd.
Vaal Reefs Exploration

MEDIUM-LIFE GOLD MINES

Agnico-Eagle Mines Ltd.
Blyvooruitzicht
Camflo Mines Ltd.
Campbell Red Lake
Free State Geduld
Harmony
Pamour Porcupine
Pato Consolidated
President Brand
Western Areas
Western Holdings Ltd.

SHORT-LIFE GOLD MINES

Dickenson Mines, Ltd.
Durban Roodepoort Deep
Geo Surveys, Inc.
Goldex Mines Ltd.
Loraine Gold Mines, Ltd.
Quebec Sturgeon River

Royal Agassiz Mines Ltd.
South African Land and
    Exploration Co.
Stilfontein
Vanderbilt Gold Corp.
Welkom

Among Research Capital's gold holdings are the following long-life South African mines: Doornfontein, East Driefontein, Harmony, Hartebeestfontein, Kloof. Libanon, President Steyn, St. Helena, Southvaal Holdings, Vaal Reefs, West Driefontein, Western Deep Levels, and Winkelhaak.

Medium-life South African mines held by the fund include Free State Geduld, President Brand, and Western Holdings.

It's difficult for a U.S. investor to pick among the South African golds. But if you do decide to shun the funds and go it alone, you might consider subscribing to the quarterly *Mining Journal*, 15 Wilson Street, London E3, England ($30 a year).

An American investor wouldn't get a stock certificate if he invested individually in the South African mines. To avoid the complications of transferring foreign shares and collecting dividends on them, U.S. investors trade in American Depositary Receipts, known as ADR's. These are substitutes for stock certificates, which are held abroad by American banks.

All of this advice is old hat to James Dines, who has consistently been recommending gold since 1961 through the medium of his newsletter. If you had listened to Dines back then and bought stock in ASA, which as we men-

London *Financial Times* Gold Mining Index*

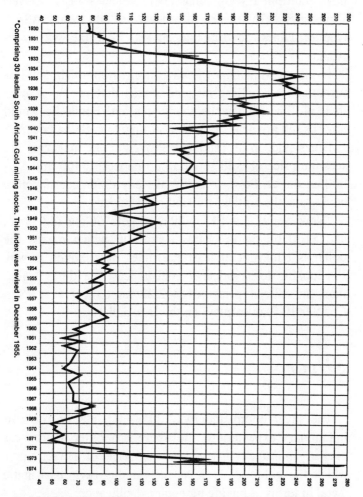

*Comprising 30 leading South African Gold mining stocks. This index was revised in December 1955.

South African gold mining stocks have shown dramatic appreciation since 1971, partly a reflection of unstable world economic conditions.

[93]

tioned invests in South African gold mines, you would have multiplied your stake about fifteen-fold. However, Dines says, "Don't worry, it's never too late to buy ASA." One of Dines' favorite slogans is, "All the way with ASA."

In effect, what Dines is advising is a buy-high, sell-low formula. He's betting on gold stocks that are at or near their all-time high while the stocks and bonds he would have us sell are near or at their all-time low. Bad advice?

Dines said, in an interview in *New York* magazine, h. sees the price of gold shooting up between $400 and $1,- 000 an ounce. So it doesn't make any difference if you're buying on the uptick, he said, and added:

"Now, we've got $11 billion of gold at the old price, and $130 billion in claims against it, which means the dollar is bankrupt at least ten times over, which is why I'm looking for a price of gold at least ten times higher than the official price [of $42.22 an ounce] ... It's a Chapter 10 [bankruptcy] on the U.S. dollar."

Silver

The silver boom underway, like gold, has its roots in inflationary expectations. But there is another factor—an alleged shortage—driving up the price of silver, upon which the goldbugs look as the number-two charismatic metal in terms of having monetary significance.

The price of silver bullion was as low as $1.96 an ounce as recently as January, 1973, and then jumped to

$6.70 in February of 1974. Silverbugs look to the metal reaching $10 or $15 an ounce within the next five years.

Supply and demand economics has had a lot to say about the silver price rise. In 1973, industrial consumption of silver was 13% higher than in the previous year.

The history of silver in the U.S. is marked by Washington attempting to control silver speculation. In the 1930's, silver had to be nationalized to prevent windfall profits for silver speculators. Another method open to government intervention has been sales from the government's silver stockpile.

In June of 1968 the government stopped redeeming Silver Certificates with silver. Now Washington has completely withdrawn from the silver market.

Meanwhile, industrial use of silver—particularly in the photographic and electronic industries—has zoomed against a backdrop of what appears to be declining silver supplies. Some government and industry officials contend, however, that the U.S. and the world have adequate silver supplies for the next decade or more.

Allan Adler of Los Angeles, one of the nation's leading silversmiths and a close follower of the silver scene, suggests low supplies of silver may allow speculators a field day. "The U.S. government is out of silver (almost; not enough is left in the government's stockpile to appreciably affect the silver market)," he says. "And basically all known silver has been discovered."

Some silver analysts estimate the world silver supply is running at a 43% deficit! And, say the silverbugs, as inflation increases, the price of silver will boom; the demand will multiply many times over as supplies are bid to record levels by industry and speculators. They point out that the two major U.S. silver bullion markets—the New York Commodity Exchange (Comex) and the Chicago Board of Trade—already are seeing silver reach its price limits in daily trading.

(An interesting twist to this speculative game is that the sons of H. L. Hunt, the late Texas oil billionaire, look delivery of 20 million ounces of silver in December of 1973 and some more in January, 1974. The Hunts have been in and out of silver since then, producing ripple effects in the silver market.)

Most silver is a by-product of lead, copper, and zinc mines in the U.S., Peru, and Mexico, and most of these companies are interested in producing their primary product, not silver.

Let's look at some figures.

These lead, copper, and zinc mines and a handful of purely silver mines produce about 300 million ounces a year in the face of industrial needs approaching 400 million ounces annually. Additionally, governments may need as much as 50 million ounces of silver annually for coinage purposes. Total silver in the U.S. goverment stockpile is only a little over 140 million ounces. The silverbugs could have a point.

Obviously, this has led to hoarding of silver coins such as pre-1965 silver dimes, quarters, half dollars and dollars which contain 90% silver. The government isn't going to be able to make up the shortage by ferreting out all of the hoarded silver coins for melt-down purposes. Therefore, until industry can work out viable silver substitutes, speculators may have a field day in the near term.

But silversmith Adler cautions that "playing silver for high overnight profits is a very risky operation." Silver "corrections" can wipe an investor out in a few days, particularly the speculator working on margin which is how the big silver money is invested.

Nevertheless, Eastman Kodak and the computer industry still need silver. So those attracted to the metal might be better off to buy it in bullion form and just hang on to it through thick and thin in the knowledge that the odds are probably on their side that—barring massive government intervention in some way—the price of silver stands an excellent chance of rising even further, if only because industry demand will continue strong against limited supplies.

We mention silver bullion, because unlike gold, it *is* legal for Americans to purchase silver bars. Or, like gold, investors can also get into silver by purchasing silver mining shares and silver coins (discussed in the next chapter).

You can purchase silver bars directly from a refiner such as Engelhard Minerals & Chemicals Corporation and Handy & Harman; from coin dealers; or in the silver futures markets. And, like gold, if you feel you should put some of the investment out of the country, then many Swiss banks will store the silver bullion for you for a nominal commission.

Veteran silverbugs emphasize that the U.S. government nationalized silver once in its war against the silver speculators, and that it could happen again. Actually, it's unlikely that it will, but it may make some investors think twice about storing the metal in the United States. That's why we mentioned the Swiss bank storage facilities.

Another good reason to store the metal outside your home or safety deposit box is that some foreign banks— say, a Swiss bank—can easily handle the buy and sell orders for you. Since you may have to move fast to make a buck in the silver market, it is probably worthwhile for you to pay the storage fee to overcome any liquidity barriers.

Unlike the Swiss and Austrian banks, American banks do not deal in commodity markets for their customer accounts. Federal law prevents banks from, in effect, also playing the role of a broker, whereas in Europe the functions of banker and broker are combined.

A few U.S. banks, however, are buying and selling gold and silver coins. Among them are the First National Bank of Chicago and the Republic Bank of New York. They will store the coins only if the customer rents a safety deposit box.

For the beginner interested in silver, it is best to avoid the silver futures market. Silver futures are commitments to buy or sell specified amounts of bullion at a designated date. Both the New York and Chicago markets trade only in the form of 1,000-ounce bars with the Comex contract (unit of purchase) involving ten bars and the Chicago contract containing five bars. The purchaser's margin or down payment must be at least 10% on each contract. There's no interest to pay on the balance, but if the market goes against you there will be a margin call for more money and you could lose your shirt overnight. It's a speculator's market for short-term gain and no place for the investor looking for long-term returns.

If you buy bullion from privately owned silver trading houses like coin dealers, you'll have to pay a commission over the spot silver price. That's the day-to-day price of the metal on the main silver markets in New York and London. And if you buy silver in the form of coins, you'll be paying a stiff premium (which we'll shortly analyze).

Why not buy directly from a silver refiner like Handy & Harman or Engelhard, the two silver-refining giants of the U.S.? Then you can avoid the middleman costs; you are buying close to the spot price and all you have to think about is how you want it stored.

An individual can buy silver directly from either of these outlets (at the time of this writing) in minimum 5,000-ounce lots (100 *ounce* bars). Neither firm likes to advertise that they sell to the public (indeed, Handy & Harman is pondering this policy) because they don't like to associate themselves with silver speculation. These firms sell primarily to industry and to the public through retail dealers, such as coin exchanges.

An Engelhard spokesman said the New York-based firm "will sell to anyone" 100-ounce silver bars with the .999 fineness of the content stamped on it plus the weight, serial number, and the name of Engelhard. For further information you can call 201-464-7000. The disadvantage to buying is that when you want to sell you have to do it yourself, and many people don't have the time to go back to the refiner or a dealer. That's where the foreign bank's commission fee for these services may be worthwhile to you.

Although there are many reputable private silver dealers, there also are unscrupulous ones who (as the Securities & Exchange Commission found out) advertised that they held customers' silver coins in a bank vault but who couldn't make delivery on demand. If you do business with a dealer it might be a good idea to take delivery of the silver and make your own storage arrangements.

Like gold, you can check the price of silver in the financial section of your newspaper, probably under commodity prices. The *Wall Street Journal* is another good place to check for silver prices in New York and London.

The volatility of the silver market might best be illustrated by this little vignette in *Financial World*, in which Robert B. Feduniak, a vice-president in the commodities division of Bache & Co. Inc., describes the seesaw ride of silver in one week in mid-1974.

> Most traders were caught by surprise when silver futures suddenly moved from the $5.20 level to more than $6.20 in the space of one week. Their surprise turned to dismay, however, when latecomers jumped on the bandwagon only to watch the entire advance, plus 20 cents more, be obliterated within eight trading sessions, as spot prices plummeted under $5. If nothing else, a quick 20% drop should drive home the point "inflationary hedges" have their pitfalls, too. The reasons for the sudden collapse were rather vague . . .*

In a nutshell . . .

Gold and silver isn't just for doomsday speculators—in

Financial World, "Commodity Climate" by Robert B. Feduniak, June 5, 1974, p. 29.

recent years it has been a good inflation hedge, particularly gold. But like any other commodity, there can be quick and violent price swings. Therefore, the beginning investor should stay away from the futures markets.

Gold bullion will probably continue to move upward in the near term (with brief downward price corrections) but nowhere near the predictions of the goldbugs.

If you are buying gold mining stocks, you appear to be better off going through a gold fund than trying to figure out the merits of gold mines yourself.

With the likelihood gold bullion ownership becoming legal for Americans, here are some ways of looking upon how to decide between the metal, gold mining shares, and gold coins.

The bullion is for the investor who sees economic disaster not far away. You can put gold bars in your wall safe or bury them in your back yard. It won't draw dividends (remember that pensioners!) but it will hold its international price and go even higher directly in proportion to the world's economic chaos.

On the other hand, gold mining shares have a financial history of appreciating at a rate 1½ times faster than bullion. So if London and Zurich gold prices shoot up 20%, you can usually bet gold mining shares (the high quality issues) will move up about 30%. And, of course, gold mining shares like any other stock, pay dividends. But like any other security, they are subject to the usual corporate perils of the day-to-day business world.

Gold coins enjoy the advantage of portability in a financial crisis. Again, they don't pay dividends, but they have been rising in price, like bullion, in direct relation to unstable world economic conditions. This area of gold ownership could feel the greatest adverse impact when gold bullion ownership becomes a reality for Americans, say observers, because gold speculators may not be willing to pay gold coin premiums when they can own the real thing in the form of a gold bar.

Silver, like gold, can be expected to rise somewhat in the near term because of both inflationary factors and strong worldwide silver demand for limited supplies. Again, the market can be quite volatile.

In purchasing silver bullion in the United States, you may want to save yourself some commission fees, charged by middlemen such as coin exchanges, by going directly to the silver refiner.

If it's good buy-and-sell liquidity you are looking for, and if you have trouble sleeping nights because of nationalization nightmares, let a Swiss bank handle your gold and silver transactions and take care of the warehouse storage details.

Doublecheck with your broker or bank to make sure you are dealing with reputable bullion dealers.

Remember—as in all investments—that jumping into what appears to be a "good thing" may in fact be a mirage in which a shortage of buyers could leave the unwary individual with a lot of devalued gold bricks. Therefore, be sure to assess the gold market in terms of world economic conditions (or consult with a gold expert in a bank or brokerage house). Analyze, for example, international inflation rates in the context that a relatively stable world economy means lower gold prices since inflation psychology plays a major role in boosting gold prices.

In short, you want to make sure there are buyers when you are ready to sell, hopefully, at a profit.

Thus far, it's been a good rule that hedging your portfolio with 15% or more in gold issues is a good bet during times of very high inflation.

Vilas & Hickey's Sinclair probably best sums up the relationship of inflation and gold by declaring that gold in real terms does not rise or fall in price. Other currencies instead, he says, have "failed as a store of value and at times as a medium of exchange." Declares Sinclair:

> Gold is simply the thermometer of the [inflation] situation and those who would blame gold for their problems fail to realize that you cannot cure the economic malaise by destroying or depressing the doctor's tools. People who find their savings declining constantly in real buying power look for what seems to them a store of value, a common standard. Gold fills that need, and their dollar, franc, and mark vote goes for it. Gold will continue to rise with intermediate sharp downside reversals as long as currencies around the world continue to inflate. There is no real upside potential target.
>
> It will simply go as high as paper money goes low. Fiscal and monetary policy tools used now to resist an impending recession will only serve to propel more people worldwide into metals and out of currency. It has happened before in history and due to man's unenlightened nature generally it is happening again. There is no other cure to the situation other than internal and external discipline and the acceptance of such required political heroism.*

*Vilas & Hickey Memorandum, "The U.S. Dollar—Gold Where From Here," by James Sinclair, February 15, 1974, p. 2.

Chapter VI

COINS BY THE LOT,
COINS BY THE BAG
—*Investing in Common*
and Rare Coins

The American gold bullionaire for 40 years had only two legal options: the ownership of gold mining shares (which we have explored) or the physical ownership of the yellow metal in the form of coinage. Because gold ownership had been illegal in the United States, there has been a boomlet in gold coin sales. And legalizing gold bullion ownership won't change the fact that gold coins still carry with them the convenience of their size. Thus, gold coin strong points are their ease of portability and storage, and that the small investor can pick them up individually for an investment of a relatively few dollars.

You have an option of buying bullion coins—coins which are valuable because of the amount of gold they contain—or rare coins. The former have a relatively low premium (*with exceptions*), the price difference between the intrinsic value and the market price of the coin. The latter have numismatic value and are sought by collectors because of their degree of rarity.

There are a couple of theories on these options. True goldbugs shun collectors' coins. They contend that the high premiums could plummet, leaving you with a nice collection but nothing that could carry you through the chaos of runaway inflation. A coin collection can't buy food, clothing, and shelter, they contend.

Collectors of rare coins point to the very strong market of recent years, during which prices of numismatic coins have gone through the ceiling.

Americans can legally own U.S. gold coins minted before 1933 or foreign gold coins dated before 1960. One major coin dealer explains that a coin should be judged on two levels: its monetary premium and the intrinsic premium. The monetary premium is the cost of the coin over its face value. The intrinsic premium involves the coin's "melt-down" value in terms of the price of gold or silver on world markets.

Among the three most popular gold coins that Americans have been investing in are: the American Double Eagle; the British Sovereign; and the Mexican 50 Peso.

Of the three, the Mexican 50 Peso is the most popular and the reason is easy to find. It has the lowest premium, about 13% over its face value.* Moreover, the Mexican coin weighs 1.2 troy ounces, therefore containing 20% more gold than the American coin. British sovereigns have a premium of near 30%. And the American Double Eagle has almost a 100% premium above its metallic value.

*Reflects the situation in mid-1974.

American gold coins became rare because those that were surrendered when Americans were ordered to turn in their gold bullion by President Roosevelt in 1933 were melted down and no more were minted. Thus, they also have become legitimate collectors' items. But many numismatic experts believe the Double Eagle is far overvalued and has been bid out of line by the goldbugs.

(The Double Eagle was produced in limited quantity in 1849 and then went into full production in 1850. This gold piece was worth $20 and derived its name from the fact that the American Eagle gold piece produced in 1795 was worth $10.)

You can compute your gold coin's value by multiplying its gold weight by the current world gold price in, say, London. Then add the amount of the premium the coin market is currently putting on it and you will have its total value.

As previously mentioned, if you are banking in Switzerland, most Swiss banks can purchase and store the coins for you. On the American market, which is large and liquid, there are a number of *reputable* coin dealers with which you can work.

We emphasized reputable because a number of fly-by-night dealers have also sprung up and have taken the unthinking investor to the cleaners. California has enacted a tough commodities trading law, and a number of other states are expected to do the same.

Thomas M. Jones, California's chief deputy commissioner of corporations, warns that investors should stay away from investing in coins through the mail unless they are familiar with the coin company. Moreover, says Jones, the buyer should determine whether he has actually bought coins or an option to purchase at a future date. "People surprisingly do not check out their investments as closely as they should," says Jones. Any wary investor should check out a coin operation with his state's equivalent of the Securities & Exchange Commission. These dealers are coming under much closer scrutiny amid increased coin speculation.

In purchasing gold coins from a coin dealer, you will probably be quoted prices in lots. So here is a brief key on what you are getting:

	American Double Eagle	Mexican 50 Peso	British Sovereign
Gold weight per coin	.96746 oz.	1.20563 oz.	.2354 oz.
Coins per lot	20	20	100
Gold weight per lot	19.3492 oz.	24.1126 oz.	23.54 oz.

Of course, you don't have to purchase by the lot; these coins may be purchased individually.

Take the British sovereign, for example, explained a major coin dealer. Its premium came to 28.56%—what it would cost you over its melt-down value. First use the gold weight of the 100-piece lot—23.54 ounces—as the multiplier with the price of gold on any given day (that day it was $157.75) and you'll get your gold value, which came to $3,713. Add to that the premium—28.56% plus 2% sales commission—and the total price of the lot came to $4,774.

That same day, the dealer said, the 20-coin lot of American Double Eagles was selling for $5,904 (19.34 ounces of gold, 93.43% premium); and the Mexican Peso was retailing for $4,300 by the 20-coin lot (24.11 ounces of gold, 13.10% premium).

There are also some interesting twists and turns to coin investment. Because Americans can't buy gold coins dated after 1959, foreign gold coins minted after that date are simply backdated. For example, the Mexican 50 Peso carries a 1947 date even though it may have been minted after that year. The Hungarian 100 Korona dated 1907 you might buy for gold speculative purposes was probably minted much more recently.

This type of coin isn't counterfeit. It is perfectly legitimate and known in the trade as a "restrike." They are coins made by certain foreign government mints that use the same die year after year without changing the date. And there's no way to tell whether such a coin was minted when it says it was, or decades later. But since you are buying the coin for its gold content rather than its numismatic value, it shouldn't make any difference to you.

Another quirk is that you can't take those Mexican gold coins out of Mexico—legally, that is—and personally bring them into the U.S. That's why it is easier dealing with a Swiss bank, which can purchase Mexican gold coins legally and then sell them to you.

There's another way you can invest in coins, and that's by the bag. This is a popular way of purchasing silver coins.

In 1965, the Treasury halted minting coins that were 90% pure silver. And as the market price of silver went up, so did the silver content of these coins—again known as the melt-down value. By 1967, the silver content was worth more than the face value of these dimes, quarters, and half dollars.

Since 1971, coin futures have been traded as a silver commodity on commodity exchanges, principally the New York and Chicago mercantile exchanges. On the New York Merc the minimum contract is for ten $1,000 bags of dimes or quarters. The Chicago Merc has a five-bag minimum.

There are approximately 720 ounces of silver in each coin bag if the coins were to be melted down. Like the gold coins, you can figure their worth by multiplying the price of silver bullion—say, $5 an ounce—by the number of ounces—720—to arrive at the value of the silver. Then you multiply that figure by the premium for that day.

Silver coin bags were running as high as $4,400 each by mid-1974.

The argument for puchasing silver in this form is that if the bottom drops out of the silver market, you still have a thousand dollars worth of coins. (And there are those who believe that during runaway inflation, dimes will be worth more than paper currency).

On the other hand, observes a Los Angeles dealer of old and rare coins, a bag of silver coins weighing 55 pounds (10,000 dimes or 4,000 quarters) has about the same value as a pound of Mexican (gold) 50 Pesos. Also, he says, "You can take gold coins anywhere in the world and there is a market."

Many coin dealers will sell you silver coins by the bag.

And, adds Deak's Kelly, "We even carry out the bags for little old ladies!"

Several profit-sharing groups have sprung up to pool their resources into coin investments. They include doctors, lawyers, and businessmen, all of whom, of course, are hedging part of their investment portfolio against inflation.

Silver is one of the riskiest of all the investments but, then, many investors believe it also offers the greatest profit potential. Some silverbugs recommend you keep your portfolio 70% in silver, 30% in gold; or 60% in silver, 30% in gold, and 10% in Swiss francs. (The Swiss franc offers less potential but also less risk, they say.)

But at least one astute professional has a word of wisdom for all coin investors: "I don't have a crystal ball and you have to be humble enough to know that you may be wrong. There are many unknown factors—whatever they may be. That is the pitfall of any investment. Along with the potential for gain, it intrinsically has built into it the risk of losing."

Gerald E. Boltz, regional administrator of the Securities & Exchange Commission in Los Angeles, warned individuals to beware of "unscrupulous promoters" who may devise elaborate schemes for selling investments, particularly in gold. Boltz declared that fraud artists could strip an investor of his entire savings and that individuals should first determine before investing if the company is registered with the SEC and the appropriate state agency.

The principal advantage for the small investor buying through coin dealers rather than the large organized mercantile exchanges is that one can purchase in much smaller quantities. You can also buy on margin from these dealers but you may find yourself paying a hefty interest rate. On the other hand, silver bullion futures bought through an organized auction market, although expensive because of the quantity involved, probably give you the fairest price.

Complicating the problems of the new investor is that many counterfeit coins have surfaced. A counterfeit U.S. gold coin is illegal and subject to confiscation. Some of these counterfeits are of good quality and consist of solid gold. Forgers of these coins make their profits from the unwary collector looking for some numismatic value. For example, an unworn $3 gold piece contains only one-seventh of an ounce of gold, worth about $25. But very few were minted and a genuine $3 gold piece in excellent condition would bring well over $1,000.

The best way of avoiding the purchase of counterfeit coins is to buy from long-established reputable firms (a recurrent theme in this book!). Additionally, you can get the coin authenticated if you are not sure of the dealer or private party selling it to you. One of the best ways to do this is to send the coin in question to the American Numismatic Association's Certification Service, Box 87, Ben Franklin Station, Washington, D.C. 20044. Send coins by insured, registered mail. The fee is $6 for coins valued at $150 or less; $9 up to $300; $12 up to $500; and a fee of 3% of a coin's worth for coins with a value exceeding $500.

Of the gold bullion coins, the U.S. Double Eagle is considered one of the most "collectable." (A 1907 ultra-high-relief U.S. Double Eagle brought a record $200,000 at a

New York auction in May of 1974. There are only 13 or so known specimens of this coin in existence.) The coin was designed by the Irish-American sculptor, Augustus Saint Gaudens, whose works include statues of Lincoln in Chicago, General W. T. Sherman in New York, and Colonel R. G. Shaw in Boston. In 1905, two years before his death, Saint Gaudens was invited by President Theodore Roosevelt to submit designs for a new coin. His design showed Liberty holding a torch in one hand and an olive branch in the other. The obverse shows a flying eagle above sunbursts.

Investing in the Double Eagle for its numismatic rather than for its bullion value and going into rare coin investment generally is far more satisfying and rewarding from a financial point of view, according to many in the numismatic profession. Among the most enthusiastic members, of this point of view are Q. David Bowers and James F. Ruddy who direct Bowers & Ruddy Galleries Inc. of Los Angeles, one of the world's largest numismatic firms (6922 Hollywood Boulevard, Los Angeles, California 90028).

Ruddy doesn't think inflation is entirely responsible for the sharp increase in rare coin collecting in the past few years (Bowers and Ruddy have doubled their sales every year since 1970). People are simply becoming aware of coin collecting, says Ruddy, which used to be the "poor sister" among investment items such as antiques, artwork, and stamps.

("Numismatic fever" can also be measured in terms of imports. The Commerce Department reports that U.S. imports of "metal coins, numismatic" more than doubled last year, to $59 million. And more than double that amount was imported in the first quarter of 1974.)

Ruddy says that only about 10% of the firm's business consists of individuals coming in and saying they are not coin collectors but want to invest in coins purely as an inflation hedge.

With rare coins, he declares, "There isn't the fast jump in price or, conversely, the downward possibility." In short, Ruddy believes the risk potential is reduced. The pure speculator, he says, should buy coins by the bag like any other commodity and forget about rare coins.

What should you look for in rare coins? Ruddy says once the rarity is determined you then look at the grading or state of the coin, which includes the condition of the date and mint marking. The same coin might be worth $2,000 in uncirculated condition and only $500 in the next lowest condition, he notes.

George A. Falcke, chief numismatist in the Los Angeles office of Deak & Co., believes rare gold and silver coins are about the best investments because they "increase in value automatically from year to year."

This position is refuted by the doomsday prophets who believe that a society in economic chaos will mean that numismatic coins will lose their premium and that only bullion coins will be of any value.

But Falcke recommends selling common gold coins during times of high inflation and saving the numismatic gold coins. During "normal" times he says your coin portfolio should be split about 50-50 between bullion and rare coins.

The gold content of rare coins doesn't make much difference, says Falcke. Rather, he says, it is the state of preservation—the grading quality—which is the most important asset. *"Fleur de coin"* is the most desirable condition—absolutely perfect or mint state.

Aside from counterfeit gold coins that have real gold content but no numismatic value, Falcke said the collector should beware of crooks who plate a coin to make it look like solid gold. For example, a silver coin may be plated gold. A way to detect this, he says, is to weigh the coin or bounce it on a table. To an expert's ear—such as Falcke's—the "ring" of the coin hitting the table tells whether it's authentic gold or a plated counterfeit. If you are not an expert, again I must stress the reliability of the coin dealer as your best protection.

On request, Deak and some other coin dealers will provide a written statement attesting to the authenticity of a coin. Such a statement, however, won't necessarily increase a coin's value or, in fact, have any impact on a coin's worth except to provide the buyer with some peace of mind.

The remarkable appreciation of rare coins is illustrated by Bowers in his fine book on collecting coins, *High Profits from Rare Coin Investment* (published by Bowers & Ruddy Galleries Inc., Los Angeles). The example involves the 1894-S dime minted in 1894 in San Francisco. Only 24 pieces were struck that year compared to 2½ million the previous year and 1 million in 1895. The reason isn't known. "Thus, one of America's most famous classic rarities came to be," says Bowers.

In 1957, Ruddy purchased an 1894-S dime at auction for $4,750. "This news," says Bowers, "sensational at the time, was quickly spread all over America by the various newspaper wire services. The result was a deluge of letters and postcards! I appeared on NBC's 'Today' television show as a result of this dime purchase."*

In 1961, Bowers and Ruddy again purchased an 1894-S dime on behalf of a prominent New York industrialist for $13,000 which was described at the time as a "runaway price"; and again the dime created a national sensation.

But the best was yet to come. At the American Numismatic Association convention in New Orleans in 1972, an 1894-S dime was involved in a private transaction between two coin dealers. The price: $50,000!†

Bowers points out that among the financial advantages of owning coins is the fact that in most countries there is no property tax levied on coin collections, and when you decide to sell your collection the profits are taxable at low capital gains rates.

Moreover, says Bowers, rare coin prices are not as volatile as some other investments; that is, they do not change from day to day. But they certainly do appreciate over the long term—from 10% to 25% a year for most rare coins.

Bowers also has the following answers to common rare coin questions.‡

*High Profits from Rare Coin Investments, p. 7.
†Ibid., p. 8.
‡Ibid., pp. 57-72.

There's no pat answer to whether you should purchase a few very expensive coins or several coins of medium value. It depends on how much you want to invest and, naturally, for those with numismatic interests, it is more satisfying to purchase several valuable coins than to save for a long period of time for one coin.

Very expensive coins are just as marketable as coins which don't cost much. The reason that the coin costs so much in the first place is because there is great demand for it. Thus, the rare coin market, says Bowers, is quite liquid. Bowers recalls that he and Ruddy purchased an 1838-0 half dollar in 1962 for $9,500. It was then resold to a prominent Eastern coin collector. In 1973, this coin was sold by Ruddy and Bowers on behalf of this collector for $75,000, a handsome profit.

How high can coin prices go? "How high is high?" asks Bowers rhetorically. He adds:

> When one considers that rare stamps have broken the $100,000 mark on several occasions (one was actually sold for $380,000) and that for a painting to realize a million dollars or more is scarcely news these days, then American coin rarities prices in the $100,000 to $200,000 range seem cheap by comparison!*

One of the most important points Bowers makes for the beginning collector or any average coin investor is to *never* buy common coins in the fond hope that they will—as if by magic—become rare.

"The best path is to purchase coins which have a

*Ibid., p. 61.

present scarcity and value—either realized or unrealized—in the marketplace," says Bowers.*

Accurate grading (condition) of the coin also is very important. Naturally, uncirculated coins command greater prices and the buyer should make sure he is getting what he pays for—and not a processed coin that simply looks like it is in mint condition.

If the collector has any questions, check with the International Association of Professional Numismatists or members of the Professional Numismatics Guild, two prominent dealers' organizations. Dealers who are members of these two groups guarantee the authenticity of the coins they sell and will refund the price of any coin later proven not to be genuine.

In his book *Photograde* (Bowers & Ruddy Galleries, Inc., Los Angeles), considered by collectors as the bible of coin grading, Ruddy says that devious methods have been developed of cleaning and toning copper coins to give them an artificial and deceptively brilliant surface. That's because early copper coins showing the original mint color are rare and command a substantial premium.

Also remember, says Ruddy, that "imperfections such as scratches, dents, edge bumps and light corrosion will lower the condition of a coin by a full grade."†

Coins should be considered a long-term investment, conclude Bowers and Ruddy, and they recommend holding coins a minimum of three to five years to realize a profit on your investment. They add that the biggest and

*Ibid., p. 62.
†Photograde, p. 8.

most consistent profits, however, are with coins held longer—10 to 15 years.

Les Fox, numismatic director of Perera Fifth Avenue, Inc. of New York believes the public still isn't aware of the fact that rare gold and silver coins have performed better pricewise than the common coins in the past 20 years.

Remember, by definition, a "common" coin is one that can easily be purchased by the lot such as the $20 American Double Eagle. A rare coin, of course, can be acquired, but not without some difficulty. As Fox explains, it might take a full month to purchase just 10 uncirculated Barber half dollars (1892-1916) at a reasonable market price.

Unlike common coins, says Fox, rare coins are not entirely dependent on the fluctuations of worldwide inflation and the price of gold. Gold is scarce, he notes, but its production could conceivably increase while demand drops. Dumping of silver onto the market could drive down silver prices for a long period of time. But with rare coins, he says, there is a limited supply and an increasing demand for choice specimens.

Says Fox:

> But the most important and convincing argument in favor of rare coin investment is this. Even when common gold and silver coins have appreciated in value, numismatic coins have done better. This is fact, not conjecture, and due primarily to the interest automatically given all coins whenever any particular coins capture the public's eye.

Fox also points to the 1976 American Bicentennial Anniversary which will see the issuance of new commemorative coinage, and which will spur even greater interest in collecting coins.

Here's what a professional collector like Fox recommends:

1. Lower mintage dates in all U.S. gold and silver series. Many of these are quite underrated and difficult to obtain other than at major auctions. And, he says, all are "sleepers."
2. U.S. commemorative gold coins, of which less than 150,000 of all types were struck.
3. U.S. pattern, experimental and trial strike coinage which are still reasonably priced.
4. U.S. bust coinage dated 1794-1807.
5. Certain extremely fine U.S. type coins.

The subtleties of coin collecting are many. Fox gives the example of the 1856 Flying Eagle Cent, of which only 1,000 were struck and which was listed in the 1957 U.S. coin catalog (called the *Redbook*) at $365 to $425 in mint condition. Today the coin is worth over $3,000. But very few collectors know, says Fox, that there is also an 1855 pattern of the Flying Eagle that is even rarer which sells for under $400 because it isn't listed in the *Redbook* yet. Should it gain recognition, he says it would shoot up to $3,000 in price!

In a nutshell . . .

Americans are taking the advice of the goldbugs in increasing numbers. That's okay if you don't go overboard.

There's little doubt that gold has been rising along with the rate of inflation from about $36 a troy ounce to as high as the $190 level. In this same period the London *Financial Times* index of gold stocks has risen by 500%. Additionally, many goldbugs like silver. And silver has tripled in value—from about $2 to $6 (and then down) a troy ounce.

If you are going to diversify into gold, and want to go the gold coin route, you are going to pay a premium over the coin's value. The value of the gold coin will move in tandem with the international gold price.

Play it safe and buy from reputable dealers.

On the silver side, you can purchase common coins by the bag, paying a big premium over the total worth of the coins, or you can buy silver bullion. Silverbugs argue that you can make a lot more money in a shorter time on silver. But since we are in this game, hopefully, for long-range protection against inflation, the smaller investor may to be better off sticking to fewer gold coins, which are easier to store than bags of silver coins. Furthermore, gold is still accepted by the rest of the world as a commodity containing immediate monetary value (whether Washington likes it or not).

You'll have to decide whether to acquire common coins for their gold or silver content or numismatic coins for their rare value.

Numismatic coins have been increasing sharply in value in recent years. The argument for them is that they have a long way to go before reaching their true value in relation to stamps, objects of art, etcetera. One argument against rare coins is that they could immediately lose their high premium if everything goes down the drain.

In the rare coin category, beware of counterfeits.

Wall Street has little love for gold-related investments. It's easy to see why. Almost always, good news for the goldbugs is bad news for the stock market, since the bugs thrive on rising inflation and a loss of confidence in national economies.

Nevertheless, some American brokerage firms have recommended gold stocks as a hedge against further inflation.

Remember, the goldbugs are no great messiahs. We've had inflation before. We'll have it again. But investing some of your portfolio into gold can be looked upon as insurance against hyperinflationary periods.

The price of gold is a reflection of our economic times. Those to whom the gold movement appeals, mainly professional people, the self-employed, and the well-to-do retired, have done well with gold in the past few years. As long as confidence is low in restoring America's economic health, investors will continue to make money on their gold investments.

Make no mistake, though, it is a highly dangerous game. Like any other commodity, one can get wiped out in practically no time.

Wilbourn Wiser, a broker with Los Angeles-based Bateman Eichler Hill Richards Inc., believes the smart gold traders got into the market at $90 an ounce and are licking their lips in anticipation of selling out as soon as gold ownership becomes legal in the U.S., and there is a temporary upsurge in the gold price.

Then, says Wiser, the number of buyers will sharply diminish, leaving a lot of would-be goldbugs holding a lot of overvalued yellow metal.

"When the last guy buys his pittance of gold," says Wiser, "he's not going to be quick enough to get out."

Time will tell whether the goldbugs have the last laugh. For the time being, though, gold bullion, gold mining shares, and gold coins rate a cautious recommendation as three related ways to hedge against inflation.

Chapter VII

DIAMONDS ARE AN INVESTOR'S BEST FRIEND
—*The Gem Market*

"Diamonds are an investor's best friend," says Erwin H. Sadow with a twinkle in his eye. "There aren't many commodities where you can always realize something plus get the pleasure of wearing it."

Sadow has been traveling the world since 1929 as a buyer of fine jewelry for America's largest department stores. Musing in his office in the Los Angeles-based May Company of California, Sadow declared: "I wish I'd gotten into diamonds and jewelry instead of the stock market."

Sadow's reference was to the fact that in the past two years there has literally been a gem explosion. The word in the jewelry trade is: all that glitters is sold. Spurred by inflation, investors are gobbling up everything from diamonds to rough, uncut lapidary stones, according to spokesmen for the jewelry industry. And, accordingly, prices have shot out of sight.

Sadow recalls that two years ago the May Company sold a flawless one-carat diamond for $995. The same diamond today (mid-1974), he estimated, was worth about $3,500.

A two-carat ruby that retailed for $2,000 a few years back has doubled in price. The jade market has recently been appreciating 300% to 1000%! Minerals and uncut semiprecious gems that used to be sold by the pound are now sold by the gram.

In short, on the average, gems and minerals have been going up as much as 50% a year.

It's small wonder, says jewelry buyer Sadow, that investors are converting their stock holdings into diamonds.

Individuals are even buying diamonds sight unseen, says Sadow. He recalls one lady who never came into a department store but simply picked diamonds out of the newspaper every time the stores advertised them. "She says this is better than the stock market," says Sadow.

"Why should our business (and that of most large jewelers) be good in this type of (soft) economy?" asks Sadow. "The only explanation is uncertainty."

But before you run out to your nearest jeweler to plunk down a bundle as a hedge against inflation, you have to know *what* to buy and you have to have good access to the market when you are ready to sell.

Precious gems include the diamond, ruby, emerald, and

sapphire. The semiprecious variety include the opal, garnet, and topaz.

A decade ago the United States was the principal market for precious stones. But not so anymore. Goaded by inflation, Americans now find themselves competing with the Japanese, Germans, French and Swiss for precious stones. Japan, in fact, is now the second largest importer of U.S. diamonds that are cut but unset, weighing one-half carat or more, according to U.S. Commerce Department figures.

From 1930 to 1937, gem values decreased slightly, but have been increasing since, reflecting the economic instability of the world. Since supplies of many precious stones are limited in the face of increased demand, prices have had nowhere to go, but up.

Sadow observes that diamonds have had a history of being sought for their value during times of political and economic upheaval. For example, the refugees fleeing Nazi Germany in the 1930's converted their savings, when they could, if they could, into diamonds which could be hidden in their clothing and personal belongings and then smuggled out of the country and resold.

Sadow and other diamond experts look for the "four C's" when they evaluate diamonds: color, clarity, carat weight, and cut. "A good jeweler will advise you on all four," says Sadow.

The name of the game in diamonds and other precious gems is quality, says H. B. Platt, the president of Tiffany's. "The biggest mistake people make is to go to wholesalers to get a bargain. You can be sure that someone who goes bargain-hunting is a pigeon, a setup. What he (the so-called wholesaler) doesn't tell you is that he is operating on a shoestring, has no capital with which to buy his stones, and doesn't have his own inventory. So the wholesaler is paying more because he doesn't own the stock and buys one stone at a time instead of thousands at a time the way we do. He (the wholesaler) in many cases is paying practically what we're selling our stones for."

Platt says that the markup at Tiffany's on a diamond is substantially under the standard retail markup of 100% "because we don't cut our prices or discount. We are a one-price house."

With the prestigious name of Tiffany behind each gem sale, the investor is assured of getting pretty much what he's paying for. This also goes for any other reputable dealer. And you don't have to spend a lot of money, either. Platt says the average Tiffany diamond sells for about $500, and that you can pick up a diamond at fabled Tiffany's for as little as $125.

But Platt and the other gem experts stress that for appreciation purposes, the investor must be prepared to spend fairly substantial amounts of cash on the very finest quality stones that he or she can afford.

Aside from diamonds, emeralds are the colored stones most in demand. And they have become rare because there are no more mines producing the finest quality emeralds. Colombia is the prime source for emeralds.

Ceylon and Burma are the predominant sources for rubies and sapphires, and strict export laws have led to a vigorous smuggling trade, say jewelry buyers.

The average investor is obviously going to have trouble taking advantage of this market. There is no organized exchange like there is for gold or silver. (A diamond futures market was attempted on the West Coast Commodity Exchange in 1972 but soon collapsed under trading problems and the complexities of the diamond industry.) And the liquidity problem is such that unless you sell your gems in the private market, you won't make much because of the big retail markup.

But the small investor might be able to get into the precious stone market by investigating less expensive rough gems and minerals. Turquoise, for example, has been increasing at about 10% a month. And a piece of turquoise can still be purchased for between 35 cents and $12. Ivory is worth as much as 10 times what it was five years ago. Malachite has been selling for $24 a pound, quadrupling its price in a year. Even a two-inch-square piece of Peruvian pyrite—"fool's gold"—used primarily for decorative purposes, may cost about $20.

Leonard Bourget of Bourget Bros. Gems and Minerals of Santa Monica, California, said prices will continue to rise. To illustrate, he said he and his brothers bought the entire collection of a rock museum for $50,000. In a year, he declared, it would appreciate to $75,000.

But there's a pitfall that gem hounds will encounter not found with gold and silver. It's called fashion, and it is a fickle imponderable that can cost you, the investor, a lot of money. Stones that are in fashion are going to sell at a greater premium than those that are considered passé. The public's taste for marquise diamonds—diamonds with a pointed oval shape—recently changed to a preference for round diamonds, particularly preferred by European and Japanese buyers. This change in buying patterns, if it stays, will hurt sellers wanting to market marquise diamonds.

Jade today is certainly an "in" investment.

Sidney Ashkenazie, one of the nation's top dealers who does about $2 million a year in jade sales, says jade has shown remarkable appreciation in recent years.

Unlike diamonds, however, there is no standard of measurement in jade—such as the carat—and so you have to rely more than ever on the reputation of the jade dealer.

The top of the line, so to speak, is imperial jade, which has an emerald-green color. Then there is white, lavender, and apple-green jade, all good investments, according to Ashkenazie.

With jade, he says, the age doesn't make any difference unless the jade has its roots in the Ming Dynasty (most jade comes from China), which precedes the seventeenth century.

Size also may have little impact on price. For example, a large piece of jade may be worth less than a smaller piece of the same type of jade. The reason: the small piece may contain a delicate carving. And therein lies something to look for if you invest in jade. The design of a jade statuette or a carving on a block of jade may significantly affect its value.

In February of 1973, Ashkenazie found a spectacular pair of 20-inch-high lavender jade panels in a retail shop in Rome. "They were the greatest thing I've ever seen in jade," he told me. The dealer was asking $100,000 for the pair, which had tremendous relief carving. Ashkenazie cabled his partner in Beverly Hills for the money, but before they could act, another dealer bought the panels for $90,-000. Two weeks later the panels were sold in Hong Kong for $270,000. In mid-1974, just *one* of the panels was on sale for $500,000. Jade experts expect the asking price of the other panel to be in the neighborhood of $1 million.

Ashkenazie says the carving represents about 60% to 70% of the value of jade and color about 30%. Ironically, although jade originated in China, the highest world prices are currently being asked in Hong Kong. An investor in the current market therefore may get a much better deal in the U.S. either through normal retail channels or at an estate sale.

If you are dubious about the jade you are buying, check with the Gemological Institute in either New York or Los Angeles for authentication.

Richard T. Liddicoat Jr., the head of the institute, said the wary individual can bring a diamond or a gem in for assessment. The institute, which trains jewelers, will tell you, in the case of a gem, what kind of a stone it is and define its color and content. With a diamond, the institute will study the "four C's." You will then get a detailed report on the stone. The fee is usually $25—a pittance compared to what the diamond and gem investor stands to lose in purchasing a worthless stone! What you won't get from the institute is a price estimate. That will have to be hammered out between you and the dealer.

Ashkenazie recalls selling a piece of jade to a Hong Kong dealer for $8,000. An American walked into his Beverly Hills gallery three months later and asked for an appraisal of a piece of jade bought in Hong Kong. It was the same jade. The dealer had resold it to the American for $14,000.

Obviously, not everyone has thousands of dollars to spend on jade. But you can invest in miniature jade touchstones which can be worn around the neck. They sell for between $100 and $1000 each (good quality ones) and, says Ashkenazie, can be expected to triple in value in a few years. "They're underpriced," he says. "The finest of these pieces come in white jade."

Ashkenazie claims that the jade market is one of the most liquid of any investment. Even though there are big retail markups, he says the appreciation far exceeds the pace of retail prices.

The Chinese are the greatest carvers of jade, he says, but what is coming out of China now is in limited supply, which is keeping the price high. Moreover, Burmese jade is in very short supply, and no white jade—from Turkestan—has been available for years, he says.

Sums up Ashkenazie: "I tell people not to buy jade strictly as an investment, even though I know it's a great investment. I personally just don't feel good when a client looks at it like it's a piece of stone (or a stock certificate!). I'm offended by that." Eventually, he adds, investors get "hooked" on jade collecting and fall in love with the art.

In a nutshell . . .

From Tokyo to Beverly Hills, everyone is investing in gems. The rise in sales is directly related to the increase in a nation's inflation rate. Japan, experiencing horrendous inflation, is witnessing its citizens paying $7,000 for a one-carat diamond selling for $4,000 in the U.S.

Supply—whether it be diamond production controlled by the family-owned DeBeers mines of South Africa or the Orient's corner on jade—is a key factor in holding prices up.

A big advantage is portability. Diamonds are easy to carry on your person.

A big disadvantage is that unlike an organized commodity market, unless you can sell to a private party you'll have to deal with a diamond retailer. You can be sure that any profit you make is a fraction of what the dealer has in mind. Jade appears to be somewhat of an exception to this, with the strongest market (and the highest prices) in Hong Kong.

The small investor can get into the gem market by purchasing rough stones for lesser prices.

On purchasing diamonds, be sure to check the "four C's"—color, cut, carat weight, and clarity.

For the investor who can afford it, diamonds are considered a better investment than other gems because they are easier to sell.

Go for quality. A diamond with inclusions won't sell for nearly as much as a flawless diamond. A scratch or a spot will reduce its price.

Beware of bargains! Armand V. Duschinsky, president of Pacific Gem Cutters of Los Angeles and a veteran in the diamond business, warns that stones can be chemically treated and passed off as diamonds or made to look more valuable than they really are. A seemingly valuable white diamond may have been dyed that color and could even fool an expert.

Stick only with reputable dealers—the Tiffanys of the trade.

If you are unsure of the stone, have it defined at the Gemological Institute.

The affluent families in countries impacted by high inflation are buying more diamonds than ever before. If paper currency collapses, would diamonds have the mystique of gold? No one knows. But maybe your girlfriend or wife doesn't care just so long as others notice how beautiful a diamond looks on her finger!

Chapter VIII

TAKING A FLYER
ON PICASSO
—The Art Market

Whether it's a commuter train carrying Wall Streeters back to their suburban lives in Westport or a packed commuter ferry boat transporting San Francisco's financial elite across the bay to their Tiburon chateaus, the chatter is increasingly turning from the dormant stock market to other forms of investment. And the phenomenon of art collecting is surely a common topic of conversation.

Art collecting in the United States isn't a big investment business compared to stocks and bonds and some of the other areas we have discussed in this book. The buying and selling of original art may not amount to more than $150 million annually, but with increased inflation, the industry has been growing rapidly. And with the increase in interest by investors in combination with a limited supply of good works in which to invest, the prices of paintings and prints have appreciated remarkably in recent years.

This sort of speculation has given rise to art-buying investment clubs and syndicates. Galleries have been set up for this purpose to find promising artists and then sell their works on a limited subscription basis.

Auction houses, such as Sotheby Parke/Bernet, are experiencing a booming business in artwork and have, indeed, expanded the art-related items in which they traditionally deal.

"The 'greater fool' theory has come to prevail," noted *Fortune* magazine. "More and more buyers have been paying higher and higher prices for paintings and sculpture with sublime confidence that there will always be someone else waiting to pay even more."*

Such demand has caused eminent art dealers to warn that the real value of paintings and the like may have been distorted amid speculative buying. There is also the warning that the unprecedented demand for artwork may have peaked and that the novice investor could be stuck with a loss if there is not enough buyer demand for his collection.

At first, nineteenth- and twentieth-century paintings attracted the "hot" investment money, and works by Monet and Picasso soared in price. But soon the art investment craze spread to modern painters as well, and a canvas by Jackson Pollock was more eagerly sought after than a stock position in AT&T.

Now the "in" investment appears to be original prints,

---

*"Invest in the Art Market? Soybeans Might Be Safer." *Fortune*, p. 201, May, 1974.

some of which were worth only a few hundred dollars in the 1950's and now bring thousands of dollars.

To be sure, however, the "gilt-edged securities" of the art world are still the old masters, such as Raphael, Rubens, and Vermeer.

What's in a name in artwork? Plenty! And it doesn't have to be the name of the artist.

In May of 1974, the household goods of a J. P. Morgan heiress were auctioned off at Glen Cove, New York. The prices were spectacularly above what the merchandise would have brought if it was not part of the Morgan estate. A kerosene lamp which Sotheby's, the auctioneer, thought might bring $10 from a sentimentalist brought $500. And a New York woman paid $29,000 for a Ming statue which Sotheby's had estimated would bring $3,500.

So a famous name associated with a piece of artwork could be worth a fortune.

To the smaller investor or one simply into art for speculative purposes, the print field might be the most fascinating place to start.

Marc Rosen of Sotheby's told me that "a large spectrum of Wall Street money management people are getting into it [prints]. People form little corporations who purchase prints for tax reasons."

Rosen, a print expert who works out of Sotheby's New York auction galleries, advises the collector just into prints to stick to the auction process, in effect, buying at the open market rate. If you do, says Rosen, you'll have little trouble selling quality prints at a profit. On the other hand, he says, dealers realize 100% markup on prints and your chances of profiting on a resale of a print to a dealer are small.

Rosen also cautions that the international print market has a lot of variables. For example, it is fallacious to think that you'll get a better price for a print in Paris when the market fluctuates sharply from block to block in Manhattan! You're gambling when you purchase an unknown— but then that's part of the speculator's risk that many individuals (with enough money to gamble) enjoy taking.

For the first time in the auction world, Sotheby's has begun guaranteeing the authenticity of the authorship of artworks sold through its facilities. There are two exceptions: paintings, drawings, and sculptures created prior to 1870; and no guarantee when the authenticity is proved inaccurate by "scientific processes not generally accepted for use until after publication of the auction catalogue."

That there is immense interest in art investment is reflected in Sotheby's volume figures which show that for 1972-73, there was a 58% increase in sales to $68 million over the previous similar time period. And 10 years ago, Sotheby's sales volume was 16% of the 1972-73 level.

Prints are created by an artist from a metal plate, woodblock, or stone on which the artist has created an etched, engraved, or lithographic image. A limited number of inked impressions are then made from the master image. Rosen points out that the investor or collector should not place too much emphasis on how many prints came from the master image to determine the future value of a print. Too often, he says, novice collectors have lost money because they only considered quantity instead of also factoring in quality.

"It is worth remembering," says Rosen, "that it is not always the more rare print by Rembrandt or Picasso that is the more valuable. For instance, two masterpieces from Picasso's 'Vollard Suite' may sell today [1974] for over $10,000, though they were printed in editions of 300 unnumbered impressions [plus artist's proofs]. On the other hand, many Picasso prints which are less effective may bring under $1,000 though published in editions of only 50 impressions."

Rosen offers the following tips for the fledgling art investor:

—Select and limit your primary areas of interest. Pick a group of artists *within your price range* and acquire as much knowledge about this group as possible.

—Acquire some background in your chosen area of concentration. This means learning the basic bibliographical and catalogue information about the artists of your choice *before buying*. Reputable dealers will supply you with catalogue information but do your own checking, too.

—Know the basic technical criteria of art judgment. These include the quality of the print impression; the condition; and the "state" of the print. This latter reference is to the fact that some prints undergo several stages before the artist achieves the desired result. Thus, some "states" of the print may be more valuable than others.

If the artist is unknown you are taking a calculated risk, and you may want to stick with more predictable profits from more well-known artists.

Signatures on prints produce special problems. Bruce L. Whyte, who owns The Original Print Collectors Group

Ltd. in New York City, observes that original prints in his collection are signed in pencil and numbered. The reason, says Whyte, is that if the signature was in ink you couldn't tell if it was photochemically reproduced and therefore might not be the original John Hancock you thought it was.

Sotheby's Rosen notes that prints were seldom signed before the second half of the nineteenth century and not even all twentieth-century artists signed their work. So the investor should find out if a given print needs the artist's signature to be of value. Picasso did not sign all of his prints, but where he did his signature commands a big premium—in some cases as much as 50%.

Beware of counterfeits. Whyte says the investor should be able to spot a counterfeit print—that is a photocopy— from an original etching, lithograph, or silk screen that is made by rolling a limited number of prints off a printing drum. By looking at the print through a magnifying glass, you most likely will be able to spot half-tone dots—as you would in a magazine photograph. You won't see these dots in the original print. Photomechanical reproductions, even if signed by the artist, are *not* original prints.

Whyte founded The Original Print Collectors Group, Ltd. (120 East 56th Street, New York, N.Y. 10022; telephone 212-753-7929) in 1972 after a corporate career. His investment group or club is offered a number of prints each month which eventually may be sold to the public if the membership turns them down. Whyte searches the world for modern graphics by both known and yet-to-be-recognized artists. He claims his prints are priced at least

20% to 30% below most galleries because of volume buying and selling.

Whyte's gallery guarantees its investors that if at any time a member decides he or she doesn't want a particular print purchased from the gallery it can be returned for at least the original price.

Whyte's members come from all over the world, joining for an initial fee of $25. Members also receive tri-monthly newsletters, written much like Wall Street investment reports, advising them of current trends in original prints and providing them with information on new artists to watch out for.

New York's renowned National Arts Club, (Whyte is chairman of the club's Graphic Arts Committee) lays down the following definition of an original print:

> —The original image should be drawn by the artist himself on stones, plates, or another medium allowing ·him to transfer the image onto paper.
> —The printing should be done by the artist or under his supervision.
> —The artist should have personally inspected each impression "pulled" and indicated his approval by signing each impression. The prints should also be numbered. A signature, therefore, is not merely an autograph but is a seal of approval.

A limited edition print represents a limited number of original impressions. After printing, according to the Arts Club, the plates or stones are destroyed to prevent other impressions from being pulled. The serial numbers on a print have no significance other than to show how many

SMART MONEY IN HARD TIMES

prints were pulled. Thus, a lower number does not necessarily make a print more valuable.

How fast can artwork appreciate? Sotheby's Ian Dunlop tells of a 7-by-9-inch Picasso painting, dated 1922, which sold for $47,000 in 1973. A practically identical work was then sold in 1974 for $65,000, he says.

Like anything else, he says, the more money you invest the greater will be your possible gain. "The cheaper things—the $200 to $300 item—may appreciate to some extent but not so dramatically."

A lot of big European money is going into contemporary American paintings, Dunlop adds. He says there are some art investor groups in Europe that are prepared to pay big prices for certain artists.

Dunlop recommends holding paintings for three to ten years before reselling. "I think it's unwise to buy at auction and then turn around and sell immediately," he says.

Here is Whyte's list of anticipated price appreciations of artists whose prints he is offering for sale:

Artist	1972	1974	Percent Change
Amarger	$ 30	$ 130	360%
Boulanger	150	300	100%
Carcan	120	200	67%
Calder	200	600	200%
Chagall	1,600	6,000	275%
Dali	300	600	100%
Garufi	60	150	150%
Hasagawa	80	160	100%
Kramer	40	160	300%
Jansem	100	250	150%
Moti	120	300	150%

Masson	100	500	400%
Miro	500	1,500	200%
Neiman	150	300	100%
Peretz	50	120	140%
Peterdi	150	300	100%
Secunda	40	100	150%
Tokita	45	120	166%
Tomchuck	50	100	100%
Tornero	80	200	150%
Tobiasse	100	240	140%
Picasso (Master Prints)	21,000	60,000	186%
Totals	$ 25,065	$ 72,330	190%*

"Many so-called popular artists of several years ago are not good investments today because they have flooded the market with photomechanical reproductions, outdoor advertisements, and magazine illustrations," says Whyte. "Their works are eventually dumped on the market when large holders see demand begin to slacken. Another problem lies with artists who achieve fame overnight and raise prices too quickly. Their works are subject to rapid decline.

"One must obey many of the supply-demand laws of the stock market in original print collecting or investing," Whyte says.

If Whyte finds a promising artist he might run off 100 prints and then destroy the original plate. "We go right to the artist source and then to the consumer," he told me.

Whyte makes offers for prints he has sold through his firm's newsletter. "We offer more money but we have very

Average percent increase: 95% per year.

few takers," he says in underscoring that investors enjoy hanging on to good artwork.

Whyte points out one other plus for print investors: Prints can be transported between countries duty-free, so if an individual ran into currency restrictions this might be one vehicle for moving one's wealth around.

Remember, small investors, the print market is one you can still take advantage of. And, unlike buying stock, you can really enjoy this investment by hanging the prints you buy on your office wall or in your home. Art also serves the aesthetic and spiritual needs of the buyer and may provide a very positive cultural contribution to your life.

Prices for original prints range from a few dollars to over $100,000. Etchings by Goya, for example, range from about $30 each for late editions to the $500 to $1,-000 range for fine first edition impressions.

The print field provides you with an insight into social history as well. The French social caricaturist, Daumier, did lithographs for satirical newspapers which were published in the newsprint editions as well as separate, smaller editions on fine white paper, according to Sotheby's Rosen. Impressions from the white paper editions generally cost only $20 to $100, while the newsprint editions cost only a few dollars each (usually available from print and book dealers). Legal subjects are especially popular and sell for prices more like $200 and up, says Rosen.

When asked what is the safest print investment, Rosen replies:

"Stay with the best works of artists whose place in history is already established. You should also bear in mind that not all great artists are great printmakers. A bad lithograph by a good artist is no more likely to turn into a bonanza than a bad stock handled by a famous brokerage firm.

"If you really like the work of a little-known artist you should buy it as an investment in your own pleasure. Whether it will go up in value is a matter of speculation."

As we saw in gems, the public's taste may have a lot to do with the value of a piece of art. A sudden shift in buying habits could leave you holding a lot of beautiful paintings or prints with no buyers. That's okay for a collector but obviously not good for the investor.

In a nutshell . . .

The price explosion in prints has been great in recent years and may offer the investor—especially the small investor with limited funds—a more satisfying market than oils.

The smart investor should do his homework, and in the field of art this was never truer. Know the good art dealers, the prints in demand, and the artists.

Strong shifts in taste can directly impact your investment. According to Dunlop of Sotheby's Los Angeles Gallery, the "smart money" in paintings has recently been going into twentieth-century works, particularly by the surrealists such as André Masson and Max Ernst. The cubists, such as Klee, and the pop artists, such as Andy Warhol, also have commanded big prices. But as a long-term investment, Warhol may not prove appealing, as satirical art has a history of fading as times change.

Rely on the reputation of a dealer and don't snap up art just because it appears to have a cheap price tag.

Liquidity may be a problem. You're better off selling privately, if you can, because of the huge markup.

Dunlop says it is difficult to say how long an investor should hold artwork before selling, but waiting at least three years is desirable. "You can't sell a painting the way you handle stocks and bonds," he says. "It's a matter of timing, intuition and locating buyers."

Beware of counterfeiting. In prints, look for the tiny half-tone dots—the mark of a photomechanical reproduction.

Be aware of market supply and demand. Do not buy an artist whose popularity has influenced him to overproduce prints and flood the market. This could depress prices for the artist's work for years to come. Therefore, acquaint yourself with an artist's work and production over the years.

The National Arts Club says that original prints by established artists have appreciated an average of 30%, on a compounded basis, between 1962 to 1972. On a comparative annual basis this is more than the stock market and some other forms of investments.

The new atmosphere in the art world bothers the aficionados of the trade. Richard Feigen, a successful New York art dealer, told *Fortune* he doesn't like what he sees.

"I've been getting a stream of calls from brokers in Wall Street, in California, in Denver, asking me how they can put their clients into art. Art has become a trading currency in their minds, pure and simple. I don't like it, but it is going to continue. What they don't realize is that art is an equally complex and far more specialized field than the financial markets, with a completely different basis of value.

"My mother hasn't been doing any better in the stock market than most people," Feigen declares. "She telephoned me to ask if she should buy a painting. I said, 'No! You'd be calling me every morning to see what it's worth.' "

Chapter IX

BOOKS, WINE, AND
BUBBLE GUM CARDS
—*A Potpourri of Investments*

There is a saying among certain collectors that you should put your stock in a good book (pun intended). But collecting rare books is just one area we will consider in this chapter. We'll also look at autographs, stamps, furniture, cars, plates, race horses, guns, quilts, wine, Japanese swords, and bubble gum cards. There is a certain common denominator to these investments. You have to have (or acquire) a certain degree of expertise before you jump in, cash in hand. And you should be aware that although many of these investments are appreciating faster than the stock market, there is no organized exchange to deal with them. You may experience a liquidity problem when you are ready to sell.

There is one other common thread running through these items that probably neutralizes the marketing problem. As the art collector and the rare coin collector of previous chapters well know, there is a great degree of satisfaction in collecting and the aesthetic value of the object may far outweigh any desire to turn a quick profit.

The list of items that people are collecting these days is seemingly endless. I've selected just a handful of the more popular (and a few bizarre) areas which—because this is a book about how to make money during periods of high inflation—are showing rapid appreciation for the investment dollar. In all cases, do business with reputable dealers who can vouch for the genuineness of their wares. Beware of bargains!

Books

"It was an exciting discovery," declared Georges Houle, head of the book department at Sotheby Parke-Bernet in Los Angeles. He had just located one of the finest American ornithological works—rarer than Audubon's great work—while examining books in the basement of a St. Joseph, Missouri, mansion in 1974. The volume by Howard E. Jones was entitled *Illustrations of the Nests & Eggs of Birds of Ohio*. It was published between 1879 and 1886 in Circleville, Ohio, measures 15 × 17 inches, and contains 68 hand-colored plates.

Don't snicker! Only 35 of the books were produced in a limited edition and a copy has not appeared on the auction market for over 25 years. According to Elliott Couse, author and researcher of ornithological works: "There has been nothing since Audubon in the way of pictorial illustration of American ornithology to compare with Jones' work—nothing to claim an equal degree of artistic skill or scientific accuracy."

The Jones book was auctioned at Sotheby Parke-Bernet's Los Angeles gallery on June 23, 1974, and brought $19,000.

Rare bird books have shown dramatic price increases, says Houle. Gould's *Hummingbirds* went from $7,000 to $23,000 in the same year. A complete Audubon book with its precious bird plates can bring $500,000. In such books the color plates and the condition which they are in play an important role in determining the book's value, says Houle.

In fact, natural history and bird books have been appreciating in the last few years at the rate of up to 30% a year, says Houle, and that's where the big investor book money is going. "There's a renewed interest in the subject and also an appreciation of the fine quality of workmanship that has gone into these books, particularly into things like hand-colored plates."

The point of it all is that whether or not your attic produces a rare find like this bird book, there can be little argument that rare books appear to be an exceedingly good investment.

"The interest in books and the value of books are taking a definite increase," says Houle. "We did not have a books department here when we opened two years ago. But the great market for books has convinced us not only to open a department, but to conduct book auctions on a regular basis."

Rare book collectors are reporting their investments are

appreciating at the rate of 15% to 20% a year and claim good rare books double in value every five years.

Don't be misled into thinking that you can easily find a rare book worth thousands by browsing in secondhand bookstores. You can be sure that the bookstore owner has been there first. But, occasionally, you will stumble on a rare book, either beautifully bound, or a first edition of a famous author or a specialized book like the bird book which was printed in a very limited edition. But by and large you should rely on quality book dealers or auction galleries where you can safely invest your money.

Houle observed that popular interest in books has lagged behind many other collectable items, such as artwork, because the average person would like to admire his or her investment and you really can't do that with a shelf of rare books.

But other factors have been at work in favor of book collecting. "French, English, and American antiques have seen their most popular period," says Houle. "Most of the great paintings are off the market. [Art collectors would debate this!] Investing in books purely as an investment is approaching heights not seen since the late 1920's."

If you want to start your rare book collection with established authors, naturally you should have a few hundred dollars to invest and plenty of patience. Let's say the outlay was almost $400 for a first edition of Thoreau's famous work, *Walden,* which two decades ago was selling for $50. Book experts believe that a copy of *Walden* may be worth more than $2,000 in another 20 years.

There are other ways to speculate in books. Spot books

that might have nostalgic value, for example. These include books about movie stars and Disneyana. Additionally, you might want to invest in contemporary authors whose reputations you think will endure over the years.

Should you choose the contemporary route, try for first editions and attempt to get the author to sign the book. Houle told me that an author's signature may increase the book's value three- or four-fold. A copy of *The Great Gatsby* (riding a crest of 1974 popularity) in a first edition might be worth up to $200, says Houle. With the paper dustjacket it could sell for up to $400. But with the signature of F. Scott Fitzgerald, says Houle, it can bring up to $800—and if there is a personal note by the author the price could go over $1,000 because it would become one of a kind.

Also watch for periods of history to become popular with collectors. Americana books on the Old West have become valuable, as have books on the American Revolution. There is also revived interest in books on nazism and Hitler's Third Reich era, with a particularly strong market reported in Great Britain and the United States.

Another good example of trends is the big interest in the past few years in books by Jack London.

Incidentally, books illustrated during the early days of photography—the 1860-70 era—also are doing well and some have shown dramatic increases in value.

Books off famous presses have special value. Three famed British presses were:

—Doves Press, 1900-1916. The Doves Bible is considered a monument to English printing and brings $2,000 on the market. Perhaps to insure the value of its books, when Doves went out of business in 1916, the owner threw the presses into the Thames.

—Ashendene Press, 1894-1935. Among other things, Ashendene is known for its fine editions of Dante's works.

—Kelmscott Press, 1891-1898. Its paper, ink, and style produced one of the finest editions of Chaucer, which currently sells for between $4,000 and $8,000.

A quality American press was Grabhorn Press of San Francisco, begun in 1919 and taken over in the 1960's by Andrew Hoyem, who renamed the firm, Andrew Hoyem, Printer. Grabhorn produced quality books on the West and Californiana with price tags between $25 and $700. Hoyem continues the fine limited edition tradition, producing, for example, a book of Ezra Pound's poetry for $125.

In the binding, look for leather, vellum, or early bindings, points out Houle, even if the book is of minor consequence. There's a current interest, for example, in early American bindings in the 1750-1850 period when the binder can be identified through a stamp or label inside the book's cover. Much of the early fine binding was done in Europe.

Although there are various book collecting trends in different areas of the world, the market is relatively stable and a particular book will bring a similar price whether it's sold in New York, London, or Los Angeles.

Houle says it isn't likely that you are going to find a fortune in your attic, but it can occasionally happen. He remembers staying at the historic Mission Inn in Riverside, California, in 1969, when the Inn's management told him they were cleaning out their cellar. Houle watched the operation and, to be sure, found six copies of a book, *Soldiers of the Cross*, published in Banning, California, in 1898. The Inn's owner thought it was a religious book. In fact, it was a valuable work on California's missions which Houle bought on the spot for 50 cents apiece. They turned out to be worth $50 to $75 each! Today, they would easily bring twice that price.

Examples of dramatic book appreciation are endless. Witness: Darwin's *Origin of Species,* $65 for a first edition 20 years ago against over $1,500 today. An early twentieth-century facsimile of the Gutenberg Bible in 1953 sold for $200 and is worth over $3,000 today. A few dollars for the first edition of H. Rider Haggard's *King Solomon's Mines* may sell for over $100 today. And on and on.

There's no denying the liquidity problem, however. Retail book dealers often take a 100% markup and you may be better off frequenting the auctions of estates where true market forces come into play (but which sometimes bid up items many times over their market value!).

Quick tips from the men who sell rare books: Try to buy older books rather than contemporary ones. Invest a little more money in rarer books than in a bookshelf of common books. Unless you are in the market for short-term gain, stay away from too many fads in literary taste.

And, as in other forms of art, you may find yourself caught up in a very satisfying pastime. A book is a beautiful investment that the collector can admire and be proud to own. It is a record of man's achievements. It is more than just a monetary investment.

Letters and Autographs

Houle also is in the market for rare letters and autographs. He recalls that "a little old lady" walked in off the street one day with three letters folded up in her purse. They turned out to be original letters from Patrick Henry, the American patriot, which brought $900 each at auction. As with books, Sotheby's checked out the authenticity as best possible. The woman was from Kansas and explained they had been lying in a box in her home for years.

Letters and their signatures may become quite valuable involving persons in science, literature, politics, and the arts. Houle advises keeping the letter or paper on which the autograph appears as flat as possible to preserve its value; also don't expose it to the light. And an envelope in which a letter came may be very important since it may be postmarked, providing the date for an undated letter.

The value of autographs can't be underestimated.

At a 1974 Sotheby Parke/Bernet auction, Lee Harvey Oswald's autograph (the accused assassin of President John F. Kennedy) brought $1,600, while President Kennedy's sold for $700. Mata Hari's (the spy) went for $350 and Martha Washington's for $1,500.

They were all part of the autograph collection of Harry J. Sonneborn, the founder of the MacDonald's hamburger chain. The signatures of presidents, writers, statesmen, entertainers, adventurers, dictators, assassins, and others brought $314,450 at the New York auction.

A top price in the Sonneborn collection was $12,000 paid for a frayed copy of George Washington's "Address to the People of the United States" announcing his retirement from public life, made in Philadelphia in 1796.

Abraham Lincoln's last letter, dated April 14, 1865, sold for $8,000. It is only seven lines long, addressed to the commissioner of Indian affairs asking for the delay of an appointment of a commissioner.

A vitriolic letter from President Harry S Truman to labor leader John L. Lewis was purchased for $5,000. Other signatures of presidents ranged from $70 to $90 for those of Dwight Eisenhower and Lyndon Baines Johnson to $9,200 for that of William Henry Harrison on a document bearing the Presidential seal.

Some other prices in the Sonneborn collection of autographs: Mary Queen of Scots, $5,000; King Edward VIII (later the Duke of Windsor) on his 1936 abdication speech, $90; Italian dictator Benito Mussolini, $70; Robert Louis Stevenson at age three, $1,100; Pancho Villa, $350; Napoleon, $250; Mark Twain, $150; Sigmund Freud, $1,600; Albert Einstein, $450; George Bernard Shaw, $475; and Eugene O'Neill, $90.

Remember, although reputable dealers and galleries can advise you on the value of your book, letter, or autograph, timing and awareness of the market mean everything. When a valuable object is being sold, chances are the seller feels the top of the market has been reached and it is time to take a profit.

The small investor can—and at times should, for the fun of it—buy boxes of books and letters blind at auction sales. Then, if you have taken the time to learn your field by talking to dealers and reading trade publications, you can settle down to the satisfying task of searching for that item of value—and hopefully feeling that indescribable emotion when you find it!

Stamps.

Stamp collecting, of course, has been a traditional favorite among individuals from all walks of life. In recent years, however, the possibilities of stamps as a viable investment has begun to dawn upon many who simply viewed philately as an interesting hobby and little else.

Here is a fascinating area where the individual with little knowledge about this particular market can set aside some cash and be assured of a steady appreciation of investment over the years.

Mike Orenstein, the manager of Superior Stamp & Coin Company of Los Angeles, one of the nation's top 10 stamp and coin dealers, observes that more and more money has been diverted out of the stock market and into the collecting of rare stamps.

Still, declares Orenstein, stamps lack the popularity of coins as an inflation hedge. The reason, he says, is their slower appreciation and that they are harder to find.

In contrast to stamps, coins (to some extent, even rare coins) are bought more for their short-term investment possibilities. And the track record of coins, says Orenstein, is more volatile than stamps. He contends that the value of bullion coins, and to a lesser extent rare coins, tends to follow the market.

Orenstein declares that stamps, on the other hand, have

a history of slower appreciation. But, he adds, rare stamp prices consistently move *upward* in value, albeit usually at a snail's pace compared to many coins.

"Quality material in rare stamps has a steady, slow, nonstoppable appreciation," emphasizes Orenstein.

To put this in perspective, though, stamp dealers point out that sought-after rare stamps have been appreciating at a rate of at least 10 per cent a year—not a bad deal when compared to, say, the stock market and other investments which have a recent roller coaster record!

If you are interested in stamps as an investment, do business with a big dealer—someone with a reputation. Any philatelic society or reputable stamp publication can advise you of who they are. Tell the dealer how much money you want to invest and, perhaps, what countries and particular periods of history interest you. Or leave all of this up to the dealer. "Trust in the dealer," says Orenstein. "You're not interested in the product you are investing in—but in the return of the product."

A controversial statement? Perhaps. But, adds Orenstein, it doesn't take an individual long to become infected with the hobby of stamp collecting—a hobby that has fascinated kings and presidents through the ages. "The exposure [of the investor] is the best thing ever for the hobby," he says. And the return on satisfaction can't be measured in dollars and cents as your life discovers a new dimension.

In structuring a stamp portfolio, Orenstein suggests for openers sticking with classic United States stamps. The collector who is not leaving the entire selection process in the hands of the dealer, should look for stamps in mint (the finest) condition.

Among fruitful investments, says Orenstein, would be two of the first commemorative issues in the United States. The first is the Columbian Exposition set, issued in 1893, a 16-stamp package which is selling for around $3,000. The second set, the Trans-Mississippi issue of 1898 consists of nine stamps worth around $1,300.

You'll notice once you get into stamp collecting that fine rare stamps are indeed somewhat harder to come across than coins because they seem to be held for longer periods of time in individual collections. Nevertheless, the knowledgeable investor can spot them at estate auctions (handled by major stamp dealers). But, note stamp dealers, you can also find rare stamps in dealer showrooms or in the private market. In coins, say some stamp dealers, much of your rare material *only* shows up at auctions.

An auction hint: A stamp might be propelled far over what you consider its "fair" price in the heat of auction bidding. But you must ask yourself if it isn't worthwhile paying the inflated price anyway. The reason is that it may be difficult or next to impossible to locate the particular stamp or stamp set you want through a stamp company in the private market.

With stamps then, pick a reputable dealer, specialize such as in classic United States stamps and remember that although the appreciation may be less dramatic than coins the downside risk also is less in combination with about the same market liquidity (buy and sell possibilities) as coins.

Furniture.

Read the *London Times.*

This fine newspaper reports auction prices at Sotheby's, Christie's and smaller dealers. It serves as a guide for buyers. In fact, the *Times* may well cover American auctions better than any U. S. newspaper.

In recent years, English furniture has shown great value, but according to fine furniture dealers you almost have to take furniture on a piece-by-piece basis. It's difficult to make a blanket statement. But the smaller investor can still get into the market. For example, a good quality eighteenth-century Chippendale armchair may still go for only $4,000.

The condition of the furniture is very important. Experts warn against refinishing valuable furniture, which can reduce its value by 20% or more. The fact of the matter is that if there is a stain on an antique table, leave it there!

And don't fall for the line that a famous personality once sat in that chair you have your eye on. You may never be able to prove it and without documents your investment isn't worth the premium.

Sotheby's furniture expert Philip Astley-Jones says just because a piece of furniture is old doesn't necessarily make it valuable. "Age is not enough," he says. It must have artistic and/or true historic value.

Generally, the small investor better know the field well when investing in furniture.

Vintage cars.

There's been a rapid and dramatic upswing in old cars in the past few years. But individuals would be wise to stay with the blue-chip values, which means that this is no league for the small investor.

Classic cars cost $10,000 or more. The American blue chips are considered by collectors to be all Duesenbergs, all Cords, the senior Packards and Lincolns, most Pierce-Arrows, all Cadillac V-16's and many V-12's, all Marmon V-16's, all Auburn speedsters, and all customized Stutzes. The Model A Ford and some of the other 1928-41 Ford V-8's also are highly prized.

The European blue chips are the Rolls Royces, Mercedes and older Jaguars and Bugattis.

The *Hemmings Motor News* (Box 380, Bennington, Vermont 05201) consists almost entirely of classified and display car ads, many with photos, and is a good place to start to learn about vintage cars and the field's dealers, appraisers and auction markets. The monthly publication has a $4.75 subscription price, third class mail.

Restoring cars is expensive and can run $5,000 and more. On the other hand, a mint condition restored car can quickly triple in value.

Take into account your storage costs and the upkeep on old cars which includes hard-to-get (and expensive) parts.

Smaller investors might get into the market through mutual fund-like operations under which the sponsors do the buying, restoring and selling.

Plates.

Beware of the limited edition ripoff. Stick with quality on fine plates that you'll mostly use for display rather than to grace a table setting. Famous artists like James Wyeth or Dali may enhance the plate's value. Respected companies include Royal Doulton, Royal Copenhagen, Lennox, Royal Delft and Wedgwood.

If more than 10,000 of the plates have been run off, it's hard to consider it a limited edition. Reputable dealers many times number the plates so you can check.

Americana will be playing a big role in several areas of investment as 1976 approaches. Watch for these Bicentennial plates and other commemorative plates in bronze, crystal, glass, silver, and gold.

What's a plate worth? Ask the Franklin Mint of Philadelphia, which not only mints coins but which in 1970 put out the first of a limited series of silver Christmas plates designed by artist Norman Rockwell for $100. These limited edition plates are now worth several times that original price.

Horses.

They're expensive. Figure on at least $25,000 to purchase, board and train a quality racehorse. And foreign buyers—the English, French and Japanese—have been running up the prices at auctions.

Or you can pool your resources in a partnership or a syndicate. But even here the price tag can run more than $10,000 a share. When the famous Secretariat was syndicated, the price was $190,000 a share.

No matter how you buy that yearling or two-year-old, make sure you have a reputable trainer and adviser and over $10,000 a year to maintain the animal.

Although the small investor can buy cheap shares of a syndicate for a few dollars, the return will be small. Generally, the experts point out that in horseracing the big money makes the big money.

Witness Charles Engelhard, the industrialist, who spent millions on race horses. He bought the famous Nijinsky for $84,000. The return: almost $700,000 in winning purses and a stud fee of almost $5.5 million.

Antique guns.

Here's a field where the small investor can have as much fun as the big money if you do your homework and specialize. Antique firearms sold by Sotheby's or Abercrombie or Jim Purdy in London can run from under $50 up to $20,000 for a flintlock or $50,000 for a pair of French dueling pistols.

Stick with these highly reputable firms and learn all you can about particular guns such as the Winchester or the Colt. Subscribe to *The Gun Report*, Box 111, Aledo, Illinois, a monthly publication which many collectors consider to be their bible. Subscription price: $10 a year. Also read Harold E. Peterson's *Encyclopedia of Firearms*.

Gun collecting is now considered in the same realm as art collecting, and the appreciation in firearms has been great. Sotheby's and other galleries can regale you with stories of guns that have zoomed in value. Like the early nineteenth-century flintlock pistol with an insurance appraisal of $1,800 which was auctioned for $20,000; or the Winchester rifle of 1866 vintage which might have brought $500 a decade ago and which recently sold for almost $60,000. The record appears to have been set at a London auction—a flintlock believed made for Louis XIII, which brought $300,000.

The 25% on average appreciation in valuable firearms over the past five years means that there are a lot of buyers now in the market looking for yet another inflation hedge. The competition is keen. Aside from your reading, be sure to frequent dealers and auction galleries to familiarize yourself with the field and their catalogues.

For your own protection get a bill of sale which states that the firearm you purchased has been authenticated. And a sign of a reputable gallery is a refund guarantee.

Hoping to make a rare discovery in an old farmhouse? It's tough, because of the spreading popularity of collecting firearms.

Quilts and carpets.

Have a field day, little investor! Sought after American quilts can still be found at country garage sales and auctions for less than $100. But prices are shooting up fast, to which pricetags in Manhattan boutiques attest. American quilts are riding the crest of popularity in Americana, which, as we saw, is also pushing books up in value. Quilts and carpets have become an "in" form of decoration for the wealthy.

A quilt is basically two layers of cloth with stuffing. Patchwork designs are popular. Distinctive and popular quilts made, for example, by the Amish might bring over $1,000.

There's still a lot of individual judgment in setting the value of quilts. Check with dealers like Sotheby's who can show you their catalogues. The Whitney Museum of American Art in New York also can be of help.

Pre-twentieth-century Persian, Turkoman, and Chinese rugs are commanding big prices but, unlike quilts, your investment must be steeper. Demand at dealers and auctions is driving up prices. Again, self-education is most important. Aside from books on textile art, study the exhibitions and collections at the Textile Museum in Washington, D.C., or other fine museums such as New York's Metropolitan. Oriental rugs costing a few hundred dollars a few years ago, may have increased tenfold in price running into the thousands of dollars.

Resale is a problem because of the 100% dealer markup in antiques and artwork. Therefore, the investor wishing to cash in on his appreciated carpet may have to bide his time until the right private buyer turns up.

Wine.

Don't. First of all, points out Richard Leland, a product manager in San Francisco for Paul Masson Wines, it's illegal to sell wine without a license. But, of course, there's little question that wine investors have been buying from dealers and trading among themselves.

Leland says the investors who made healthy profits are those who bought good French vintages in the 1960s.

The liquidity problem notwithstanding, a few wine collectors are able to get the word out that part of their cellar is for sale. The buyer might be a new wine collector or a restaurant which may not have been in business in the 1960's and needs a good wine base from which to build. "If you are starting a new restaurant, there is simply no way you can buy old clarets from the mid-1960's," says Leland. "And your wine list is incomplete without the French clarets."

The clarets from the Bordeaux region of southwest France have easily tripled in value since the 1960's. The Bordeaux region has long been considered France's most important wine region. During an average harvest this area produces about three times as much wine as France's Burgundy region.

Wine is classified by growth: the six top vineyards are the first growth; the next 20 are the second growth; the next 50 the third growth; and so on.

Oenophiles generally agree that the following chateaus* (in alphabetical order) have the finest Bordeaux wines: Cheval Blanc (St. Emilion); Haut Brion (Graves); Lafite Rothschild (Medoc); Latour (Medoc); Mouton Rothschild (Medoc); and Petrus (Pomerol).

In terms of Bordeaux quality, 1966 was rated excellent, while '64 and '67 were considered good. But '63, '65 and '68 weren't up to snuff, according to wine experts.

The Burgundy region, lying southeast of Paris, is con-

---

*Quality wines will carry the name of specific vineyards, or chateaus, where the grapes were grown. These vineyards or chateaus many times are owned by one individual or a family. The districts, such as Medoc, are in parentheses.

sidered much more difficult to judge and, as a result, many investors prefer to stay with the Bordeaux wines.

Leland gave an example of a common pitfall that the wine investor can fall into. The year 1970 was a good year for Bordeaux wines, he says. You could buy at the uninflated price of between $100 and $150 a case. Today, this vintage would sell for about twice this price a case. But watch out! The 1971 vintage was twice as expensive as 1970 and the quality wasn't as good, says Leland. And the 1972 vintage was even more expensive and the quality still declined. "But people kept paying the high prices because they didn't know at the time that the wine wouldn't sell because the wine was still sitting in the casks in France." (Wine investors order wine through their dealer before it ever reaches U.S. shores. The retailer orders through the particular chateau.) As a result, wine retailers may have huge inventories of these years, scaled from about $50 a bottle for the 1970 vintage.

Leland expects that wine prices will continue to come down as a result of the recent poor quality years, that the store owners will take losses, and that investors who put money into the 1971 and 1972 vintages are losing out.

"The time for investing in wine is over," says Leland.

Louis Gomberg, like Leland, a San Francisco-based wine expert, says the serious wine cellar owners—who have cellars stocked with wines worth over $100,000, and there are more around than you would guess—don't wait for a U.S. merchant to offer a wine. "The chances are they will go to Europe and bid at their favorite chateau or castle," says Gomberg. And then the wine will be routed into the U.S. to the owner's cellar through a licensed importer. With a U.S. vineyard, however, you generally have to deal with a retailer and place the order, Gomberg says.

Gomberg adds there is a growing recognition among wine connoisseurs that some California wines also improve with age. In the U.S., the American counterpart to Bordeaux wine is Cabernet Sauvignon; and the counterpart to Burgundy is Pinot Noir. Cabernet ages the best of the two, he says. Some of the finer California wines include the following vineyards:

Beaulieu
Inglenook
Charles Krug
Louis M. Martini
Paul Masson

Wine appreciation means that a $10 bottle of Chateau Lafite of 10 years ago would sell today for $150; a $2.50 bottle of Beaulieu Vineyard Sauvignon of 10 years ago is worth about $30. So there has been a corresponding increase in the value of French and California high-priced wines. They have appreciated proportionately.

(Tracing the appreciation of a particular wine is a fascinating exercise. A '59 Lafite went for about $37.50 a case in 1960. In December 1966, the well known New York wine shop, Sherry-Lehmann, listed '59 Lafite at *$194* a case. Five years later, the price was *$695*. During the Christmas 1973 season, Sherry-Lehmann was asking *$1,450* a case and it could probably be currently sold for over $2,000 a case.)

Gomberg reminds the fledgling wine investor that reselling wine "is a para-business that has no foundation in law" and simply can't be done in any state without a beverage license.

Japanese swords.

"Everybody's gone crazy collecting these swords."

That's Willis M. Hawley of Los Angeles speaking, one of the country's leading experts on the Japanese or samurai sword.

The samurai made a fabulous sword and, indeed, the samurai sword collector is a fanatic among collectors. For the investor, if you can find a *genuine* samurai sword, you will, to be sure, have something in great demand and which is a good bet to appreciate in value over the years.

But the pitfalls are of major proportion!

Who were the samurai? The Japanese character for samurai also means scholar. The samurai, who were a product of a Japanese feudal system until about 1870, were just that—gentlemen and scholars whose spartan training produced a military officer of the highest mental and physical caliber who worked in a lord's private army.

The swords these samurai warriors produced are legend. They are almost always curved and the steel blade is among the sharpest of any sword ever crafted.

Production of these swords goes back to the year 900 with most of the quality samurai swords last manufactured in 1870 when the Japanese feudal system crumbled. There are some quality samurai sword craftsmen left in Japan—but very few.

So sharp, strong, and well made are these swords that

they have been tested by slicing off half-inch metal pipes without nicking the blade! There is a machine gun on exhibit in a Tokyo museum which had its barrel severed by a samurai sword.

There is much legend surrounding the samurai sword which feeds its popularity among sword investors. Collectors of samurai memorabilia like to tell the story of one of the greatest samurai warriors who lived in the 1700's. The warrior had stopped for lunch at a roadside teahouse only to be challenged by three ruffians who wanted to provoke him into a Western-style shootout so that they could steal his fabled sword. The warrior ignored the insults and kept eating his rice. After the insults got more vicious and menacing, the warrior simply picked up his chopsticks and crushed four flies buzzing near his face—in midflight! The three intruders quietly left. The physical prowess and discipline of the samurai warrior was nothing to be tampered with.

Sword expert Hawley and Martin Lorber of Sotheby Parke-Bernet's New York gallery agree that collecting or investing in samurai swords is an extremely complex venture.

One of the biggest pitfalls is that of the counterfeit signature of the artisan. Since the maker's John Hancock on a sword is of prime importance in determining its value, and since there have been some 18,000 samurai craftsmen in Japanese history, this obviously is no easy game for the layman.

Hawley estimates that as high as 90% of the signatures of the great Japanese samurai swordmakers on swords in the United States are counterfeit. He should know since he has compiled two volumes on the swordmakers, has one of the biggest libraries on the subject and is secretary-treasurer of the Southern California Japanese Sword Club which has worldwide membership.

It's very difficult to spot counterfeit swords," says Hawley. "That's one of my jobs."

Hawley tells the story of a group of samurai sword experts from Japan who gathered near Los Angeles to appraise some 2,000 of these swords. One sword offered for sale by an Englishman for $5,000 was deemed counterfeit by the panel and was subsequently sold to a collector friend of Hawley's for half that price. The friend was convinced, however, that the signature was genuine. Upon checking Hawley's reference library it was indeed found to be genuine. It had fooled the experts—a clear warning for the would-be investor.

These swords sell from a few dollars to several thousand dollars each. A recent Sotheby sale brought $70,000 for a single samurai sword. (Incidentally, samurai collectors have been sharply critical of auction galleries like Sotheby's and Christie's for allegedly "driving up" the prices of these swords to what they claim is far beyond their real value. Moreover, claim collectors, price speculation by foreign buyers has caused many prized samurai swords to end up in collections outside of the United States.)

A few hints on investing: Remember, it's the swordsmith not the age of the sword that usually matters.

The handle may add to the sword's value because of its gold or silver inlay work.

Look to the private market before you begin dabbling

in auctions. It's difficult to find individual samurai swords for sale, but they have been turning up, says Hawley, in newspaper classified ads. You might have to go off the beaten track, adds Hawley, remembering that some samurai swords have been uncovered in rural communities. Therefore, he says, keep probing small town newspaper ads for a collector who is in the market to sell.

There are a few signatures to look for among living Japanese swordsmen. Miyire and Sadakazu are among the valuable names.

As was the case with jade prices being higher in China where it is produced, you may find better prices in the United States than in the Japanese market.

Moreover, the market can be very volatile. Japanese (and some other) samurai sword speculators found they had to take a big loss in the fall of 1973 during the Arab oil embargo. At the time, Japanese speculators were heavily investing in artwork and other types of property in an effort to get rid of their inflation-eroded yen.

When the energy crunch hit the Japanese economy the bottom fell out of everything, including Japanese swords, which fell to a quarter of what they had been selling. Once again, however, the prices of these swords are making a comeback.

In conclusion, keep in mind the complexity of the market. No two samurai swords are alike which makes pricing difficult. It also is hard to spot a counterfeit signature of the craftsman (remember, though, that the fake, if of good quality, may have its own value, albeit much less than if it was an original).

Try to keep up with some of the literature in the field,

although most of it is in Japanese. *The Art of the Japanese Sword*, by B. W. Robinson and *The Samurai Sword*, by John Yumoto, are two good English language reference works.

The zanies—bubble gum cards.

Aside from monetary profit one should, to some extent, enjoy the investment. And if it's as crazy as collecting bubble gum baseball cards—well, there are no bounds to the delirium. In fact, for some it's just like investing in stocks and bonds. No kidding!

Dwight Chapin, a sportswriter for the Los Angeles *Times*, tells a story about Bill Haber, a New York card collector who located a rare 1910 card with the picture of Honus Wagner, the great Pittsburgh shortstop. Wagner had ordered the card off the market because it showed him chewing on a plug of tobacco and, the story goes, Wagner didn't want youngsters to know he used the stuff. Haber wrote to the six or eight collectors in the U.S. who he knew had a Wagner card. Finally after being turned down by each of them, Wirt Gammon, a Chattanooga, Tennessee, sports writer, and one of the best known bubble gum card collectors in the country, said he'd sell his Wagner card. Although it was creased and stained, Haber said he borrowed $350 from his wife and bought it. Haber declared that by mid-1974, the Wagner card had appreciated to $1,500!

Topps Chewing Gum Company of Brooklyn, New York, turns out the little pasteboard cards of thousands of baseball players. Stan Musial, Joe DiMaggio, Ted

Williams, Jackie Robinson—all the greats had their pictures plastered on the cards, which are 2½ × 3½ inches.

Topps produces 500 million sports collector cards a year, generating $33.8 million in revenues.

Haber says a New Jersey man took his money out of the stock market and invested it in "mint" 1957 Topps baseball sets. "He got 35 sets, put them in a safety deposit box, and is just letting them lie there," wrote Chapin.

Fanatics abound among the baseball card collectors. Larry Fritsch, a 37-year-old Wisconsin resident has 11 million cards which fill a 30-by-60 foot steel frame building on his 70-acre farm. Fritsch is now in the business full-time, selling a million of the cards a year.

In a nutshell...

Here are some guidelines for our potpourri of investments:

In all cases, seek out only reputable dealers who guarantee to the best of their knowledge what they are selling you. Quality dealers allow you to return the merchandise in a short period of time if you are not satisfied.

Do your homework. Read books in the field, join clubs, and visit museums and galleries specializing in the area in which you are acquiring knowledge.

Don't believe that prices have nowhere to go but up. As we saw in wine, a lack of buyers leaves you holding the bag—or in this case the bottle.

Limit the amount of money you wish to invest.

Because of the liquidity problem with many of these in-

vestments—that is, the difficulty you may encounter selling a book or an Oriental rug—don't think you can cash
in your investment as quickly as a security. There are no
organized exchanges or central marketplaces. Thus, it may
take a little time to turn a tidy profit.

Be able to spot trends which can impact your investment.

Watch out for so-called bargains by fast buck operators.

Chapter X

A LAST WORD

There's no question that inflation is going to continue at a relatively high level for the indefinite future. It's a built-in factor in our economic system. The big questions—to which no one, including the present Administration, has the answers—are for how long and to what degree?

Perhaps the government can get a grip on the economy and the runaway inflation many dread won't happen. In any case, since most thinking people see enough inflation in the near term to make life miserable for the average worker trying to stretch weekly salary, you ought to think about some of the investments we have discussed.

It's certainly not too late to hedge some of your savings against inflation's erosion of your earning power. At a minimum it would be wise to put as much of your money as you can comfortably afford into short-term money market instruments which, with the exception of commerical paper, contain a minimum of risk. In this way, you will at least be neutralizing some of the double-digit inflation of the 1970's.

Then, with a little extra cash, you can explore the more exotic investments such as those which are gold- and silver-related, or artwork.

There is a general rule of thumb that as the rate of inflation climbs the individual should hold less and less cash. Inflation just eats away the purchasing power of cash lying dormant in a bank or savings and loan account and should be put to work. Set aside what you need for your daily expenses, enough for a short-term emergency, perhaps enough cash equal to three to six months salary, and then begin looking at the investments we have talked about which tend to appreciate during times of high inflation.

Moreover, watch your spending habits. Shop with care, picking out the sales and bargains at discount stores. Refrain from panic buying just because there are rumors that particular products are going to jump in price. It makes good sense for your pocketbook. And it makes good sense for the inflationary impacted U.S. economy in which a dampening of demand could have a salutary effect on rocketing prices.

Much of this book dealt with commodities such as gold and silver. Like all commodities there is the sudden downside risk as well as the opportunity for great gain.

There are two attitudes toward commodity investing. You may want to gamble everything in the thought that we're heading for a crash anyway. So if you lose everything in the attempt to make a killing, it won't destroy your ability to build your finances for another try.

Then again you may be among those who see flaws in the way the U.S. economic machine is operating but you don't see disaster lurking around the corner. Thus, you may want to invest only that money which is discretionary and which you can afford to lose without putting a crimp in your finances.

After you determine your financial objectives—both immediate and long-range—then analyze the various forms of investment to meet these objectives.

For example, foreign money in the form of the Swiss franc and other "hard" currencies would be expected to provide solid short-term gains if you let them appreciate for about a year or more.

Indeed, maximum short-term gains could come from speculation in silver or currency futures, but the risk factor is high.

If you want day-to-day liquidity don't tie up your money in bank certificates of deposit.

If you want safety, hedge some of the more speculative investments with securities backed by the United States government.

Real estate, artwork, and rare coins and stamps might provide you with substantial long term gain.

In a moderate to high inflation all the investments in this book would apply.

But if you feel everything is about to go down the tube, you might want to switch predominantly into the doomsday havens of gold and silver, cushioning such investments with bags of silver coins which the gloom and doom school feels could be the only currency in a crisis. The author doesn't see this sort of economic calamity on the horizon, however.

Always keep in mind the liquidity factor. Will you want to cash in on some of your investments on short notice? Assess the market to make sure it is as easy selling as it was buying.

Beware of the temptation to use too much leverage in commodity investments. You may think putting out only 10% margin (down payment) on a commodity is a bargain. But if that commodity plummets you'll owe a lot more money. Get the facts from a reputable brokerage house.

Think in terms of the unconventional as well as the traditional ways to invest. It's the innovative money that makes it first and then the flock follows. Even in the stock market, for example, over-the-counter stocks may prove better risks than listed securities during times of high inflation. Dynamic small-growth companies might provide greater income than a so-called blue chip.

By all means try to enrich your life by enjoying and learning about some of the investments in this book. The ability to expand your intellectual horizons outweighs short-term monetary gain.

You can take advantage of inflation and make it work for you. The Age of Inflation demands new approaches to living and investing if we are to continue to enjoy the world's highest standard of living.

If the proposals in this book provide you with a little

extra income during the fight against inflation, then it was all worthwhile.

Finally, buy the best that you can afford in any field. History tells us there's no substitute for quality, and it's quality that shows the greatest appreciation.

And remember, it is axiomatic with any investment to learn as much as possible about your field of interest. In that way you'll ultimately be able to depend on the instincts of the person in whom you have the most trust—yourself.

Caveat emptor!

INDEX